FORAGED FLORA

A Year of Gathering and Arranging
Wild Plants and Flowers

LOUESA ROEBUCK
SARAH LONSDALE

photography
Laurie Frankel

TEN SPEED PRESS
Berkeley

CONTENTS

Each thought that is
written
has as its reflection
a trail
within the heart
of the forest

Song of Heyoehkah
—Hyemeyohsts Storm

INTRODUCTION

My faithful dog, Scrap, is lying in my lap as I write this.

Her name is Scrap, and she's a Chihuahua / dachshund / terrier mix. She weighs 17 pounds, not an ounce of fat on her perfectly athletic and graceful body. She is perhaps the most intelligent animal I have ever rescued and I've been bringing home strays since I was four. She is unusually swift of foot and can jump almost five feet from a standing position. She obsessively hunts rats. She is inquisitive, charming, elegant, and sassy enough; possesses a healthy soft coat; is clear-eyed and obedient to a fault; loves cheese more than she loves me, and, I think, is perfect.

Why am I going on about my dog?

Because she's a rescue from South Central LA.

She's not a Labradoodle from Australia bred to be hypoallergenic,

nor a sleek but high-strung-sensitive pointer meant to work game birds in a field for pleasure. She's not an imported Irish terrier, or a Norwich . . . or a French bulldog that to my mind mostly serves as a design statement.

She's a "mutt"—do people still use that word?

From a rough part of town with a rough start, who found us through friends and has made our home complete.

I love her dearly.

This is how I approach my floral life and work. Indeed how I have since I was that same four-year-old girl bringing home strays and blooms for my mom.

There is endless beauty and bounty all around us, right in front of us, waiting to be seen and embraced and taken into our homes, if we can only see it.

I am fortunate enough to now live in California, a place of astonishing fertility and abundance. At any given time in the calendar year, in my very modest cottage yard, or on the paths my daily life takes, I see flora that beg to be seen and or brought inside.

Pick Me Please.

I don't want to list these now, that's some of what this book sets out to do: Record just a fraction of what is abundantly growing, blooming, fruiting, and even elegantly dying in every month, in the ecosystem I inhabit.

Why on earth would I desire peonies flown across the oceans from New Zealand (out of season)? Why would I wish to purchase winter narcissus in July, or lilacs in September? Or why would I want poppies in NYC in the early fall? Or exotic Japanese ranunculus flown to my floral shop in California?

Why, when the earth always offers something perfect right here, right now?

I strongly believe this desire for the "exotic," the unusual, the rare and difficult to cultivate, the bloom from the "Orient" or another continent, arose in eras and civilizations now long past and, I hope, beliefs long past.

It was a display of wealth and power to give one's chosen lady a heavily scented gardenia from another land, another season. It was a luxury that few could obtain or afford. (I believe we as a planet can't afford these luxuries anymore.) There was less romance and prestige in an apple blossom from the kitchen orchard or forget-me-nots gathered by the stream. A sweet bunch of fresh nasturtium blossoms held less import, as did wild heirloom roses gathered with your own hands, and no gentleman would offer bright blue borage blossoms or thyme gone to seed, bunches of fennel mixed with Queen Anne's lace, or even a perfectly formed magnolia branch.

I think this is all backward. There are miracles of the natural world around us daily. Romantic, unexpected, and overlooked, beguiling, elusive, and sometimes "invasive" flora that we can and should bring into our homes and environments and offer each other with love.

I am discovering more and more as we live this way—as we eat almost all of our fruits and vegetables from a 20-mile radius, in season, and as I create floral work with the same ethos—that what is most beautiful and most fitting is what grows together in the same time of the year, even of the month.

I notice the blackberries tangled with the 'Cecile Brunner' roses, and then (thanks to a long-ago human hand) a stray hydrangea with perfect antique patina. I cut them as they grow along the road and create an arrangement that closely honors how they grew. I might add jasmine if it's looking healthy and vibrant; it will look and smell sweet in the house.

As I drive north through the Olema Valley on a winter errand, I see in the fields bright red, yellow, and saffron willow growing wherever there is water, striking against the emerald bay trees and the haunting usnea lichen–covered oak, with their silver-gray mantles. Some years if we are lucky there are bright red toyon berries. I'm not a holiday person, but I can't help but think this is where solstice and then Christmas garlands and decorations stem from—the land—and how perfectly divine it is to me in these fields and valleys I call home.

As we enter a new year, the yard becomes alive with brilliant acid green nasturtium leaves, wood sorrel with electric yellow blooms, and huge borage leaves and peppermint-scented leggy geranium. There is always a rose survivor or two that I can add to the bedroom mix. And I am always ecstatic to see the year's first magnolia blooms! Deep magenta or, close on their heels, the magnificent Campbell magnolias with their huge cup-and saucer-blooms, pale cream tinted the palest pink imaginable. We may even have some cobaea vines producing moody deep-purple flowers.

February brings redbud, more magnolias, and plum blossoms everywhere with their sweet happy scent. March brings lilacs and wisteria, and on and on and on.

Louesa

hyper-seasonality, but we wanted to articulate it in a much deeper way, working with and photographing what we found throughout the year, utilizing only what was at hand.

We set out to create this year of arrangements, limiting ourselves to materials either foraged—flora gathered from open, public spaces—or gleaned—flora gathered from the surplus harvest from a garden or agricultural land. We reached out to friends and acquaintances whose homes and creative spaces would best reflect what was in season. This allowed us to illustrate how responsive and aesthetically connected the work is to each unique environment.

This book also comes out of a deep love and gratitude for California. We are both transplants to this state and greatly appreciate its temperate climate, and rich, fertile, and expansive land. The state's natural abundance offers a wealth of resources for foraging and gleaning—even in year three of a historic drought. But the philosophy that underlies this book is universal and can be applied wherever you live—the idea of truly seeing and thus better understanding the landscape.

Several years ago Louesa and I collaborated on a few articles featuring flowers and plants Louesa had foraged from backyards and roadsides near her home in West Marin, California. Her installations and arrangements were very organic and free form, dynamic and fun. Foraging is an ancient practice, but despite this history, her work felt ahead of its time, radical even. It was something Louesa had been doing for years

Observing and gathering what is around us is a natural extention of the concept of eating seasonally and locally, a belief we both subscribe to, and we wondered what it would look like to document a whole year of foraging flora. We were interested in the concept of

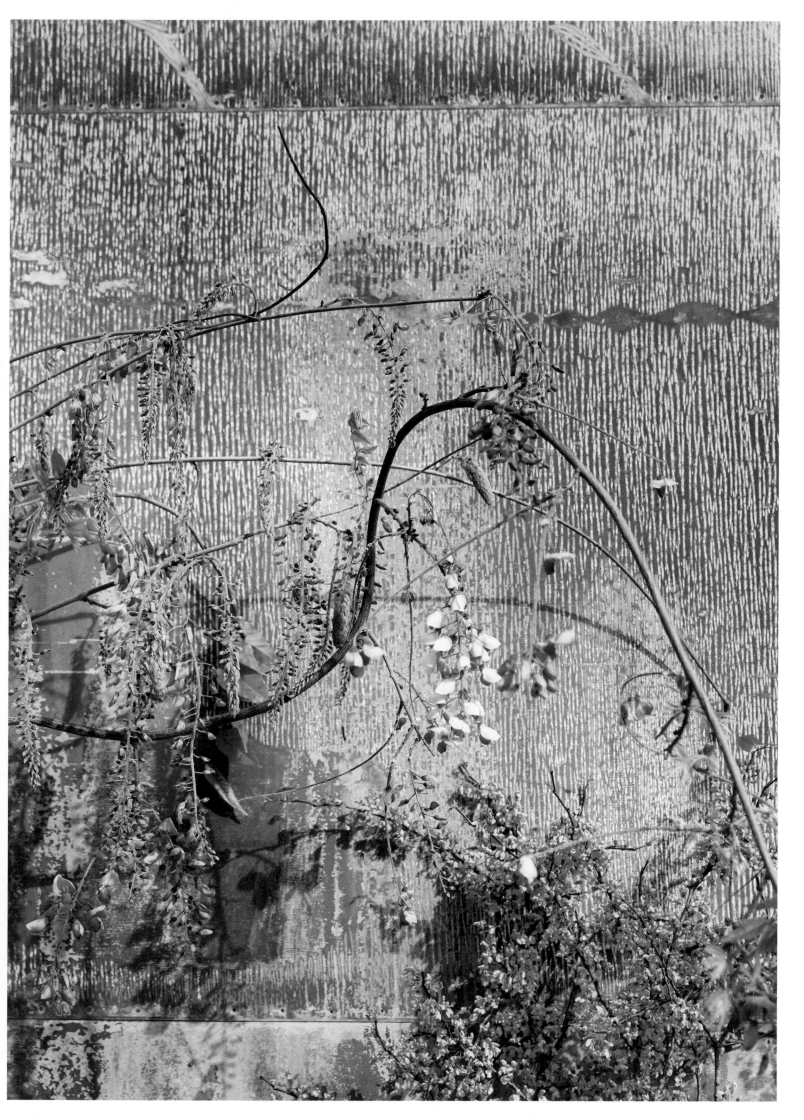

As a child in England, walking to and from school I would award points to gardens in my city neighborhood (apparently editing was in my bones from an early age). When I was eleven, our family moved to the country, where, much to my horror, my urban landscape was replaced with a view of rolling hills and sheep in the far distance. Yet the memories that have stayed with me most are of the thick English hedgerow, picking wild blackberries at summer's end, and dodging nettle thickets at the bottom of the garden. For all the experiences we may accumulate in life, I think these primal memories are the ones that root us most to our past.

In my twenties I lived in Tokyo for almost a decade. I had yet to visit the United States, and Tokyo was my introduction to towering skyscrapers. The city was a wonderful mix of dense, modern concrete urban jungle and traditional wooden houses and neighborhood temples, the old and new packed together so tightly and physically so close it required a different form of seeing, a more micro view of the world. Several pots lined up outside a house became a garden; a single blossom heralded spring. The Japanese celebration of the four seasons only heightened this way of viewing the world; across the culture, small cultural signifiers greeted each season's arrival. The minutiae of everyday life were rife with poetic overtones.

When I later moved to the U.S. West Coast, the scale was jarring and, after Japan, completely disorienting. Everything was so big—the food, the cars, the people, the homes. Suddenly the micro was meaningless and often felt ugly. It was the big vistas that

were beautiful: the large swaths of landscape, the long sandy beaches, and the endless horizons, revealing the curvature of the earth. I had to step back and literally see the bigger picture. California seemed to be all about scale and the macro.

I got to know Louesa through years of living in the Bay Area—I still own several cherished pieces of clothing she sold me—but our first collaboration was decorating an event space several years ago. She trucked in piles of foraged bay laurel and fennel; I knew them by sight, but in working closely with them, I slowly began to notice the smells, the textures, the forms. After the event, I started to see fennel and bay everywhere—in gardens, in fields, lining the roadside. This was neither a micro nor a macro adjustment but simply my visually tuning in to my environment. I could just see more.

When we later worked with magnolias, which once had seemed so awkward and unattractive, they now seemed extraordinary—and like the bay and fennel, they were everywhere. How had I overlooked them before? It wasn't just seeing up close that had changed for me; it was my new ability to step back and see the full landscape not only in its natural, geographical context but also in the cycle of the seasons. This was a much more holistic, primal way of seeing. The more Louesa and I worked together, the more I learned to see and appreciate flora that for so long had been right in front of my eyes, but invisible.

Sarah

FROG'S LEAP

SEPTEMBER

The terrain had been changing gradually as they traveled, and, unconsciously, Iza recorded each detail of the landscape they passed through, noting especially the vegetation. She could discern minor variations in the shape of a leaf or the height of a stalk from a great distance, and though there were some plants, a few flowers, an occasional tree or shrub she had never seen before, they were not unfamiliar. From a recess deep in the back of her large brain she found a memory of them, a memory not her own. But even with that tremendous reservoir of information at her disposal, she had recently seen some vegetation that was completely unfamiliar, as unfamiliar as the countryside. She would have liked to examine it more closely. All women were curious about unknown plant life. Though it meant acquiring new knowledge, it was essential to immediate survival.

The Clan of The Cave Bear —Jean M. Auel

fennel · allium
roses · hydrangea
figs · grapes

Pristinely pruned vineyards, European inspired wineries, and decorative fountains can distort your vision of the Napa Valley as you drive up Highway 29. However, there are still pockets of the old agricultural world with farmhouses, water towers, and wooden barns that recall the valley's simpler, agricultural early days. One of the most iconic of these holdouts is Rossi Ranch, north of Rutherford, named after its owners, Rachael and Fred Rossi, who spent more than a century here from 1906 to 2007. The very first vineyards were planted on this land in 1866, and the vines have been continuously farmed ever since. The land, now in a conservation easement and owned by Frog's Leap Winery, is home to John and Tori Williams, and is where we headed in early September for our first shoot, our cars loaded with fennel and allium. We drove slowly up the dirt driveway, careful not to kick up dust onto the grapes that are hanging plump and heavy, hours away from being picked. Harvest had just begun.

Our good fortune was to be foraging the gardens with Tori, who showed us the barn, with its turn-of-the-century wine-making gear and wooden wine tank on wheels and tracks, largely untouched since the forties. Although we had planned on shooting at another location, we seized upon the opportunity to use this space, with its industrial/agricultural vibe, and it quickly became both a refuge from the searing end-of-summer heat and a majestic, gritty backdrop for showcasing our finds—fennel and allium—in all their glory.

Sarah

FENNEL, FENNEL, FENNEL, FENNEL

The tallest fennel I have ever found. We cut a few wagonloads on the ridge road that travels between Bolinas Lagoon and the northwestern slope of Mount Tamalpais, above Stinson Beach, carving a path south toward Mill Valley. Late, late fall fennel, before the winter rains. The deer— does with twins, and young velvety bucks without mates—like to eat all bits of the fennel and then take shelter under or beside it, creating nice soft circles on the ground.

A small estuary, a tributary of Bolinas Lagoon, provides enough water for the fennel to thrive nearly all year long, and the heat of Mt. Tam enables it to grow tall—8 to12 feet at least. Incredibly healthy with no road debris or pollution to dull the plant.

We were surrounded by many honeybees feeding (we thank them); no stings.

Sarah picked up equally tall, healthy, dramatic and I'd say unusual leeks, *Allium Porum* 'King Richard' variety from farmer Bob Canard. His leeks were sculptural and unexpected, just wonky and curvy enough . . . big like the fennel.

They still had a tint of very pale celery green, papery and cement-like in tone and texture, exquisite with the fennel, the first time I had used that combination.

Bulbous ends and curves that gave a feeling of fertility in the fall. Seeds, thousands of seeds waiting to be invasive in the best possible way. Invasive seeds that yield endless variety of edible uses. They are just barely cultivated; they don't really need our feeble help. We carried them home and planted them the following February. They will reach this stage of maturity in eighteen months . . . full circle from seed to full height just in time for the publication of this book. Sarah used her dried leeks to create a privacy barrier in St. Helena and will plant the seeds.

After the shoot we drove them into S.F. and offered them to my friend Sylvan for the Buddhist blessing of his restaurant, Rintaro.

Louesa

There was moody cinematic light filling the space, coming in through two huge sliding barn doors and high slit windows, invading the cool darkness just so. As we settled into our secret cave, it all became better and better.

Cement plinths on the barn floor became an architectural element, almost Donald Judd to us all.

The shoot took on a northern European/industrial vibe—not the cliché wine country backdrop we all knew we wanted to avoid.

Vast ceilings and ladders tall enough make me very happy. We quickly and rather easily created a 12- to 20-foot scrim of fennel and leeks, suspended upside down of course! The tallest, most serpentine allium imaginable . . .

A worthy companion plant for the grand and pristine fennel. I have hung dozens of vertical, suspended fennel installations, sometimes on their own, and often paired with other blooms. The palette of the allium, fennel, and cement was sublime, and dictated these huge compositions.

Scale became distorted, also
my preferred state of being, just
a touch of the psychedelic.

Was it huge? Was it tiny? Who can tell?

The idea was to take the same ingredients from the large installation and break them down into smaller compositions.

Fennel is perfect for this. It's a perfectly agreeable plant (I'd even call it a flower). It looks interesting at every stage of its life, it's amazingly hardy . . . you can only do damage to it when it's young and tender and brilliant verdantly green. You can break it down to any size or dimension and it behaves. It offers solid architecture and structure by itself or as a form to add most any flora to.

Back to the endless virtues of fennel. Its fronds are lacey and strong and brilliantly chartreuse, citrine, bronze when dying, or pale, pale wooden gray depending on the time of year. And it smells divine!!!!!!!!!! Of warm summer hikes, and anise cookies fresh from the oven, of roast pork in Sicily, of ayurvedic toothpaste, everything clean and warm and aromatic. When I use it in installations people uniformly have a primal and positive reaction to the scent, one of strong memory.

To me it's a medicine in addition to a food . . . and a thing of great beauty. I never tire of it.

Most florists now throw too much in with this clean perfect plant, I prefer just a few good companions.

The pale blue pharmaceutical glass vessels I love and cart from site to site seemed not quite small enough, but sometimes materials dictate. The fecund, continuous, recursive fractal leek heads and the healthy Mt. Tam fennel just fell together; they fit. I didn't need to do much. That's the best sign.

PAIRINGS

Roses marry well. Hydrangea is exquisitely balanced with it in both of their lifespans. Wild dark grapes, the more unusual and gothic the better—those are a great look with fennel and hydrangea.

Always odd numbers in everything never even. So then if we added fig, we need an unidentified vine . . . that makes five elements. And we are done—oh no, we forgot the leeks!

Most often if a composition works very big, even oversized, it's likely to be interesting very small. I'm not that interested in the middle ground. This holds true of almost all areas of life for me, of landscape, of flora. The most challenging environments are the middle ground—suburbs, mid-sized cars, cultivated roses all cut to the same height, even mid-sized vessels.

I gravitate toward the very large, oversized—or diminutive.

But we may return in the spring . . . stone fruit
blossoms perhaps, or wisteria.

My own foray with fennel began with Louesa when I first saw it hanging upside down in bundles in her Oakland store, August, in 2006. Almost a decade later, I hired her to decorate a large, soulless, empty office building one winter for a Remodelista event. She arrived with carloads of aromatic bundles of bay and fennel that she hung from the beams and pillars, visually transforming the space but also infusing it with a heady scent of bay that wafted through the air. At the end of the day I took one of the fennel bundles home and hung it outside my front door. Over the ensuing months it slowly dried out and then, to my amazement—as if this act of nature was some sort of miracle—the dried-out flower heads cracked open, spilling the seeds onto the ground. I collected them as they fell, then later toasted them, sprinkling them on food and grinding them into salt as I relished having witnessed this small act of nature.

Sarah I think of fennel as one of your go-to materials, a workhorse of sorts—what's the draw?

Louesa Fennel is glorious in all its stages. I love it at the end of the spring when it is super velvety and brilliant green and grassy, feathery and furry. Then I like to use it when it's dying and drying out—it's a very different vibe. Fennel is good in a drought, and it will tell you where your water sources are. It's weedy and wild and is everywhere if you look for it—I never feel bad cutting it. And it has big culinary use. At Frog's Leap we used it at the very, very end of the season. It's over as soon as the rains come in early fall.

Sarah Fennel wrangling tips? How do you work with such oversized greenery?

Louesa I do an initial cut to hydrate but I don't cut things down until I start arranging. I don't ever want to lose height. People tend to cut their materials down too short and they lose scale, proportion, and compositional opportunities.

Sarah How do you arrange when you are dealing with oversized elements?

Louesa One of the big mistakes is when there is not enough negative space. People work with clumps, and that can lead to bad composition. Look at each branch as a separate element—isolate each one and see each bloom. You can't see anything when it is in a clump bundled together. When everything is a distinct element you can build a composition.

Sarah How do you create a flow?

Louesa If you have a big pile of fennel moving, leaning, or bending in one direction, keep it as is . . . work with that. I've really learned that however something falls, to just keep it that way, let it flow. You cannot create nature. Learn to get out of the way or work gently beside nature.

I would leave
them for up
to a month.

They look
beautiful as
they dry.

I take them down
when they gather
too much dust
or when they
are washed out
and faded.

Sarah Not everyone has the space to accommodate large installations. How do you break down big elements like fennel and leeks and create smaller arrangements from them?

Louesa If I am working with large pieces of fennel or leeks, I cherry-pick the components that have the most interesting shape, color, and curvature. I'll then cut them down to the length I want, but I'm careful of not cutting too short or too quickly. When building a small or medium arrangement, only cut to the new scale once you have all the materials together.

Sarah What combinations work with fennel on a small scale?

Louesa I like to mix it with hydrangeas, and roses. The fennel becomes a very different element when used on a small scale. Something useful to note is that the structure of fennel makes it really versatile and is essential for holding the roses and hydrangeas without using cheating elements like foam.

Sarah How do you work with leeks, which like fennel have a lot of length but have a very different form?

Louesa The leeks were extremely sculptural to me and had a wonderful strong form all on their own. I didn't do anything to the leeks for this installation but simply arranged them in the chimney pipe we found in the barn or hung them in their original state with the fennel. I didn't cut the leeks down or try to pair them with other flora. I wanted to see them as a singular element, placing them one at a time until the piece felt complete, and retained a good amount of negative space. It was a true compositional decision.

Sarah Is there any secret to tying the fennel or leeks when you hang them?

Louesa The trick is that you don't want to tie too high in the stalk or in the middle of the stalk—it's not good compositionally, as you have all this end. Tie them as close to the bottom as you can where you cut it. I go over and around something and do a fishing knot. It helps to find things to latch on and weave string around. The irregularity helps. The middle pieces can fall out easily, so tie it tight. People tend not to have a strong enough hand, so make sure it's actually secure without breaking it. There is a little sweet spot where it is tight and secure but is not mangling the materials.

I have a collection of twine and string that I seem to carry from gig to gig. It spans the gamut from pedestrian hardware store sight line string in neon green, orange, or pink, to antique waxed linen on spools I probably paid too much for in Petaluma. If I see twine or string I dig in my travels, I buy it and store for the future. They always get used, and it's not a good thing to source on the fly.

Sarah How long would you leave the fennel and leeks hanging?

Louesa I would leave them for up to a month. They look beautiful as they dry. I take them down when they gather too much dust or when they are washed out and faded.

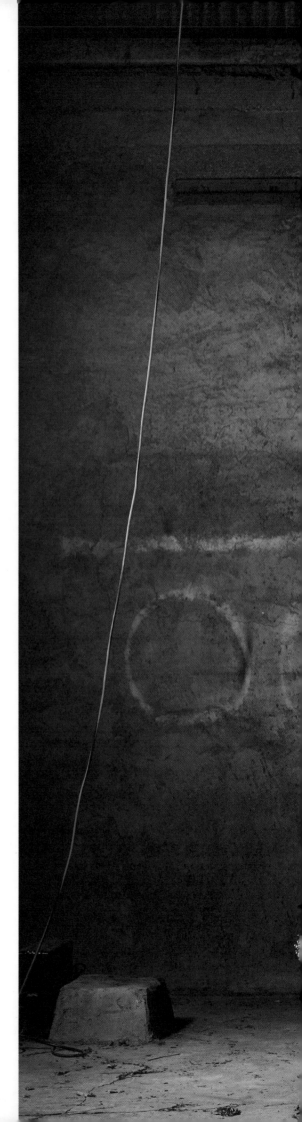

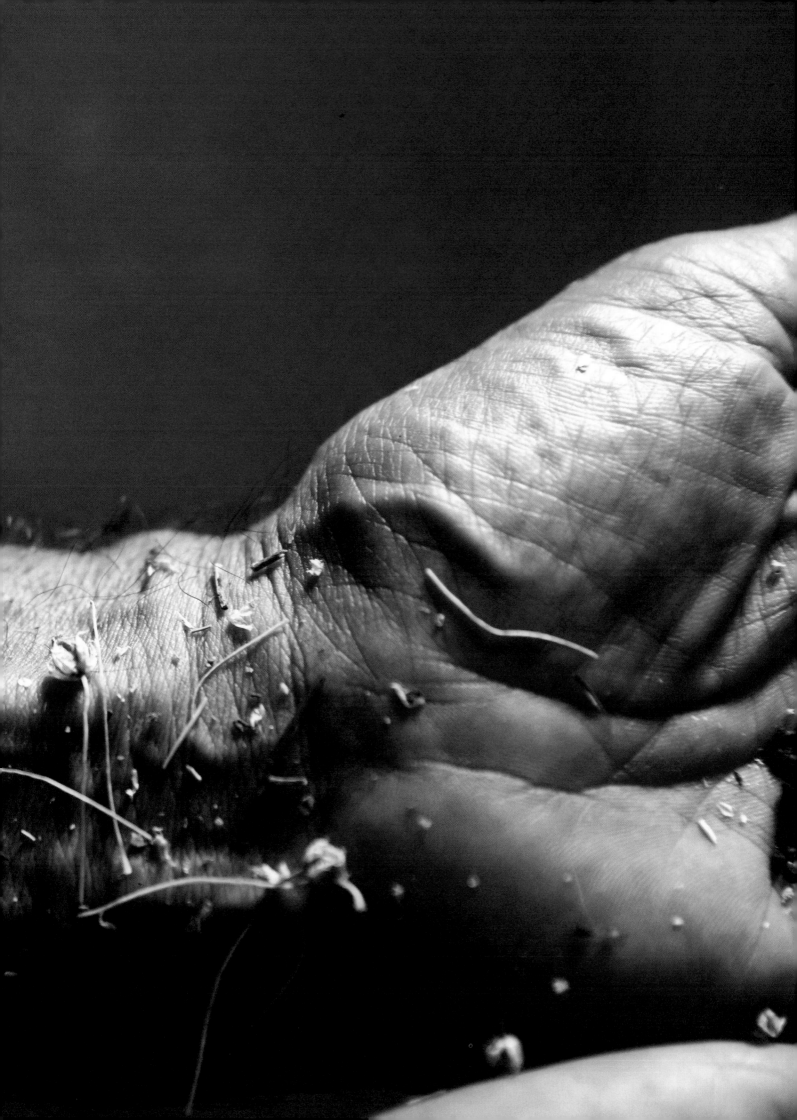

SEASON OF MELLOW FRUITFULNESS

OCTOBER

"The harvest is over," declares the mother one day. "There is enough food. We deserve a rest."

But before they desert the meadow for the year, there is something else that has to be done . . . The two women are holding torches made out of bundled grass. They touch the torches to the meadow. The grass crackles and sputters around them as the flames creep along the ground, heading toward the oak-bay forest. The heat becomes more intense. The women now drop their torches and hurry along the path . . . they feel happy once again. The harvest is in, and it has been a good year . . .

As for the meadow, it will lie blackened and desolate throughout the summer. Then, when the first rains come in October seeds in the ground will germinate again; by the following spring the meadow will once more be a rich source of flowers and grasses.

The Ohlone Way — Malcolm Margolin

hops · roses · quince · persimmon
fennel · pear · tomatillo · fig · amaranth
basil · mint

Just as dawn was breaking on what will prove to be a blisteringly hot day, we climb out of the Napa Valley and dip over the hill into an adjacent wooded valley. We wind our way down almost to the bottom before turning off into an unmarked driveway and bump along an unpaved dirt road toward the home of artist and ceramicist Richard Carter. As we narrowly skirt a huge boulder that sits perilously close to the edge of the road, I spot the creek below that has been temporarily dammed for the summer to create a swimming hole, a much-needed refuge from the heat. Just before we arrive at Richard's century-old farmhouse, we pass an orchard of fruit trees planted over a hundred years ago, their boughs laden heavy with persimmon, pomegranate, and quince, their burnished skins ready to burst and their color seductively vibrant. Although autumn is in full swing, the summer heat has yet to subside.

I have been to Richard's farmhouse many times, but the view of his ranch as you turn the final bend never fails to remind me of a simple Japanese farmhouse that has been left to weather in time. The house and surrounding barns, now converted into studios, sit on 85 acres nestled above the creek, an area once home to the Wappo Native Americans, signs of their existence still evidenced in rocks with holes carved out as mortars in which acorns were once ground. Built in 1903 by the prior owners, the farmhouse remains relatively unchanged, its rustic look having been painstakingly maintained and crafted by Richard with aging patinas preserved, wood stripped bare, and weathered imperfections embraced, quietly showing the passage of time with its effortless rusticity.

It's against these surfaces that we document October's bounty. Although Louesa has filled her car with lengths of heady scented hops, it is outside in the kitchen garden, a shameless cornucopia of seasonal offerings rife with the gentle hum of bees, where herbs and roses are gleaned for the table and fruit gathered from the nearby orchard for the creation of our tribute to harvest.

Richard's studio sits in a restored wooden barn, one of several on the property. A large rusted corrugated tin roof structure nearby houses the kilns. Although we had planned to shoot in the farmhouse, it's the primal nature of the kilns that draws us in, and it's here where we stage the first installation.

Sarah

One of the most interesting and beautiful traits of Northern California is how the hottest moment of the year happens just before the cool winter rains begin.

We drove to Pope Valley, a place of astonishing and almost wild beauty, to capture my interpretation of late harvest.

The three-year-long drought was in what looked like the middle of its path. The day would be 101°F in the shade, testing human and plant endurance.

Hot bright days yield hot bright colors—too-sunny yellows, garish oranges, dahlias in nursery school primary colors, dry purple zinnias, flame reds, and candy pinks with no blush. These colors make it into my arrangements sparingly, or never.

Instead, we harvested quince and persimmon in Richard's orchards, and in his kitchen and bountiful ornamental gardens, herbs going to seed and amaranth, and as always, it seems, there were roses.

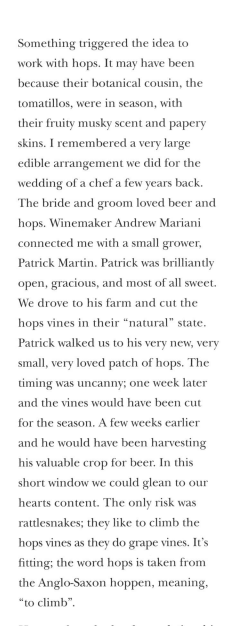

Something triggered the idea to work with hops. It may have been because their botanical cousin, the tomatillos, were in season, with their fruity musky scent and papery skins. I remembered a very large edible arrangement we did for the wedding of a chef a few years back. The bride and groom loved beer and hops. Winemaker Andrew Mariani connected me with a small grower, Patrick Martin. Patrick was brilliantly open, gracious, and most of all sweet. We drove to his farm and cut the hops vines in their "natural" state. Patrick walked us to his very new, very small, very loved patch of hops. The timing was uncanny; one week later and the vines would have been cut for the season. A few weeks earlier and he would have been harvesting his valuable crop for beer. In this short window we could glean to our hearts content. The only risk was rattlesnakes; they like to climb the hops vines as they do grape vines. It's fitting; the word hops is taken from the Anglo-Saxon hoppen, meaning, "to climb".

Humans have had a close relationship to hops for a very long time. But they are rarely seen as decorative, so we took these to Pope Valley to adorn the kilns and farm tables.

Louesa

We cut as many vines as we could without feeling piggish—I guess we could have cut more. There is an addictive quality to this work. I always desire more—and worry, will there be enough? Do I need more? The first time I saw Richard's property in Pope Valley I was struck with intense ancient associations—Etruscan, or North African. I must have had these visions still rolling around when I prepared for this shoot. I think my single favorite aspect of creativity is how these subconscious or barely conscious memories, or experiences, often come forth without effort. During the installation and the two-day shoot I wasn't thinking that I wanted an Etruscan look, but that is certainly what the hops, persimmon, amaranth, and quince ultimately conjure. Was it the old grains and fruits, cultivated for centuries?

Perhaps I rambled aloud about North African art to Laurie; she certainly captured the golden, ancient, fertile harvest I imagined.

The long-distressed but sturdy blue farm table in the screened-in porch at Pope is terribly romantic and old-world feeling. It gently provides a sense of the garden beyond the screens and the tidy warm kitchen directly behind. To me it's distinctively masculine, a gentleman's high country porch, meant for farm lunches or elaborate dinners for honored guests. This shoot was defined by hops, so in keeping with that guiding element I began to lay the spine of the table with the long rope of hops, keeping the easy curvature of its natural form.

I started as I usually do with the spine of the structure that meanders in a snake-like fashion from end to end and then over the edge. I begin to place the small rose and herb arrangements and fruits. I never begin in one spot and work in a methodical manner. Here, I looked for pockets in the vines to place the roses, the quince, the herbs, and the persimmon. Each element placed helps inform the next and the next, and usually gets more obvious to me and, I guess, easier. It's a process of hopping all around the table, pausing occasionally to step back a few feet and judging the composition color relationships and texture. Occasionally as you build this composition it will become obvious that one of the elements is discordant. For instance, there was beautiful overripe pomegranate in the garden the days we shot. But once placed on the table they didn't work. Removing is just as important as adding.

Hops were historically an important crop in Yolo and Sonoma Counties, but for various reasons were gradually replaced with other more lucrative crops. It's been decades since fresh hops have been grown and been available to California brewers. Fresh hops have many qualities superior to frozen commercial hops, not the least being scent.

Our farmer, Patrick, is also a big advocate for the medicinal and nutritional properties of hops, not just for getting mildly buzzed. Fresh hops contain more of the essential oils, possessing a bitter aromatic taste and a strong characteristic, which I quite like. I also think they have a mildly calming effect when you handle them.

Hops have tonic nervine, diuretic, and anodyne properties. We all know they have sedative effects and often promote a healthy appetite and sleep. They have been employed for nervousness and insomnia. Hops-stuffed pillows have been used for centuries to treat insomnia.

Hops were consumed not just as beer or ale but also as tonics, tinctures and vegetable bitters, a cheaper and less intoxicating way to receive medicinal benefits. It is the female hops flower, which is globe shaped, that is used by brewers.

Patrick also shared with us an interesting culinary fact. Hops shoots are a prized delicacy, more expensive per pound than truffles, white asparagus, or roe. He would love to educate the Bay Area food-obsessed community about this little-known morsel, full of nutrition.

Putah Creek grows Chinook, Cascade, and Centennial varietals of hops. Patrick shared the nuances of each: Chinook was redolent of citrus and pine, Cascade more grapefruit, Centennial a bit of resin.

We left feeling energized and educated, and a bit odd. Our car was delicious smelling—warm and fruity and a bit boozy. Sarah may have suspected we were buzzed—we were a little, I guess.

We were on high hops alert for this shoot, as Louesa was madly compelled to find them.

Sarah I like how you kept some of the hops with the string still attached; you can see how they grow vertically like runner beans.

Louesa I kept some on the string and took others off. It's more beautiful to have a mixture, but including some of the string was interesting and felt more autumnal. Hops, like clematis and passion flower, already have a vine structure, but they're easier to work with on the string.

Sarah How do you like to go about decorating a table?

Louesa One way is to build the table down the center first, then lay down plates, linens, silver, and glassware. The second is to know where everything goes ahead of time. For a dinner party or wedding, I like to have everything laid out first; it helps dictate the table and I can map it out. I don't want my imprint to be too big and later have to subtract. In this case the hops are the spine; then I added the fruit—quince, pear, and tomatillos—and then the prepared rose arrangements.

Sarah You typically build your pieces in order, each step intuitively dictating the next. Is this the only time you make small arrangements ahead of time?

Louesa If I'm doing a dinner for, say, sixty people or more, I'll build little pocket-size arrangements before the main structure. I decide what elements to use—like roses, herbs, and blossoms—then lay out all the vessels on a flat surface in a line and build the little arrangements with the agreed-upon ingredients. Next, I build the bone structure, the definition of the table. Then I place the little arrangements where the table tells me—I intuitively feel and see where they live. I'll go back and retweak, adding a rose or a bit of quince to each arrangement. It's a back-and-forth dialogue between the little arrangements and the bone structure.

Sarah Anything else to consider?

Louesa Where people are sitting; if I can, I'll get the guest list ahead of time. You always have your heroes, like roses or magnolia—your floral money shot. It gives me joy to place those where the bride or the mother of the groom or a guest of honor is seated and can see them.

Sarah What pairings do you like?

Louesa Blackberries, currants, and fennel. Little edibles like thyme and oregano. What looks beautiful growing next to each other in nature typically tastes good together. It's companion planting, something I learned at Chez Panisse. If blackberries and jasmine are growing beautifully together, I'll use them on a table.

Sarah How do you create movement and flow in your table pieces?

Louesa Some people make one thick column down the center. I prefer to create a meandering creek with little tributaries, thick in some places, thinner in others. I put the small arrangements in the pockets of space, which also help for placing glasses.

Sarah In your arrangements, the flora are never truncated but always seem to float off the ends of the table.

Louesa I love tendril-y materials like passion flowers and hops. The trailing tendrils are one of the most beautiful parts of the plant, and I like to let them naturally meander off a mantelpiece or fall twirling off a table.

Sarah It rounds off the table so beautifully.

Louesa People have a lot of fear about leaving something hanging off the table—they worry something is going to get caught—but it's poetic, and it's the prettiest bit, and there is gracefulness in that—it adds a lightness.

Sarah In your vertical structures you like to go for scale, but here you keep everything low.

Louesa In this one area I follow the rules: think about the guests before your arrangement. I learned the hard way when I created arrangements that were too high and were annoying to the guests. I learned to keep it low, low, low.

Sarah You keep it low, but you still have movement.

Louesa You can have more movement when it's low with a bunch of little arrangements. Rather than three oversized arrangements, you can use twelve small ones; it feels more symbiotic with the food.

Sarah With small arrangements, what do you look for in a vessel?

Louesa Something with a wider mouth. If the opening is too small, it's worthless. Many potters make ceramics for one stem—too small for an arrangement. The sweet spot is a nice open squat mouth.

Sarah We ended up using tall ceramic cups at Richard's.

Louesa How could we not use ceramics at Pope? They are so primal, and they were everywhere.

Sarah Any rules for using fruit?

Louesa With any edibles on a table, avoid clichés, so it's not just a bowl of fruit. Use whatever is in season. Try and find fruit with stems and leaves, or a cluster of fruit. Here we brought in fruit from the orchard, but you can use store-bought or from a farm or farmers' market. Just avoid the shiny polished pieces, and look for hyper-seasonal fruit that's misshapen and maybe with a few worm holes.

CHINATOWN

NOVEMBER

Today it rains all over the world
and you and I are birds
imagining the security of the nest
the pillow beneath the head
the branch of basil on the window.

Angel in the Deluge—Rosario Murillo

magnolia · passion flower · roses
clematis gone to seed · rose hips
hydrangea · violets

Building a floral arrangement or creating an installation is very much like painting, and Louesa often talks in terms of line, composition, color, and negative space. With that in mind, our good friend, cookbook author and photographer Heidi Swanson's Quitokeeto studio in San Francisco's Chinatown proved to be the ideal blank canvas with its clean, minimal look, freshly painted all-white walls and wood floors, and two empty shop display windows, begging for flora.

It was a dank, drizzly November day when we arrived early and started unloading the car, packed to the brim with magnolia, passion fruit, roses, hydrangea, and more. Louesa wasted little time in covering the floor with the magnolias in an effort to separate their forms, each flower a snapshot of nature caught in a different stage of bloom, some with petals flung open to the world, others tightly shut, reluctant to emerge, and then every stage in between. Small-to-medium-sized arrangements were displayed in groupings in one window, creating a wave of color from deep reds to creamy whites and dusty pinks, while in the other, vines suspended from hooks transformed it into a green passion flower jungle of sorts.

As we were preparing to leave Heidi's at the end of the day, looking back at the rich visual tableau of flora created with its diversity of color, it was hard to imagine that this was November.

Sarah

November is an awkward month. The rains have yet to begin; we are beyond the golden still warm months of late harvest, with overripe fruit and bronzed flora. But happily there are still some scrappy survivors here and there. The wet, lush, and colder period of "winter" lies before us, with its abundance of healthy green.

When arranging these in transitional months, more thought needs to go into flora foraging and selection.

I made a preliminary list, as I always do. I usually stick to about half and deviated on the rest.

Here's what was on the list.

Roses and rose hips, ferns and fern tendrils (too early, it turns out), late late herbs, passion flower vines with blooms and fruit, clematis gone to seed, Michelia magnolia and pink Japanese Magnolia x soulangeana, Magnolia liliiflora, and Yulan magnolia.

And then under my list I usually jot down some notes that are free-form.

Moody grandmother

Tokyo sci-fi pharmaceutical glass

Heidi Swanson's Minimal, minimal White on white

Very feminine with a tiny bit of androgyny

Vines and tendrils

Louesa

HEIDI SWANSON'S
MINIMAL, MINIMAL . . .
WHITE ON WHITE

VERY FEMININE WITH A
TINY BIT OF ANDROGYNY

VINES AND TENDRILS

Occasionally, or more often if you are listening to your intuition, timing can be uncanny. We went to SCRAP, a wonderful resource for artists of all sorts in San Francisco. SCRAP is a center for reuse, and a source for cheap and unusual props and working materials. Just as we were walking in the door, a donor dropped off an unusually large collection of pharmaceutical glass, a tremendous score! Hours later and it would have been scooped up. This find defined the vessels for this shoot.

The glass was paired with Heidi's thoughtfully curated vintage culinary objects and neutral ceramics for a bit more texture. These collections also determined the scale of our arrangements. None of the vessels were large, so we were playing with small to medium arrangements, which could be clustered together for volume.

I intuitively began building and arranging, as I would have in any of my past shops. Heidi of course has a perfect assortment of objects, both immensely practical and just beautiful. She also possesses a clean feminine aesthetic that greatly defined my choices.

It seemed natural to work with a creamy tawny palette including burnt salmon roses, romantic passion flowers, and of course magnolias. I knew she would appreciate the clematis gone to seed for its fluffy, fiber-like lacy form.

MINIMALISM VERSUS MAXIMALISM

Minimalism versus maximalism.

There is no "less-is-more" with Louesa, something I quickly learned and slowly came to appreciate. At Heidi's we decided to document the layering of flora on her white shelves to show how to build a display and also to reveal the depth and richness that each layer adds. The first layer was a simple composition of clematis gone to seed, mixed with blackberry stems, and for me, the minimalist, seemed perfect in its restraint. For Louesa, however, this was just the beginning. Densely petaled butterscotch roses in myriad hues were added to the center of the display, mixed with rosehips and hydrangea, bringing a richness of color to the monochrome palette. Once again I thought we were done, but Louesa pressed on, adding a whole new layer of magnolia to create a rich lushness that transformed the piece into a multidimensional installation. Sometimes more is more.

Sarah Talk me through how you layered this piece

Louesa Like any architecture, begin with good bones before you add the fluff. I usually start vertically because the tall pieces create space and structure. If you start with big branches and vines you can create the height first, then cut them down. This was very much a vertical structure to begin with, then I added the horizontal elements. With the vines, I first placed the long ones to create space and add structure, then added the smaller tendrils at the end.

Sarah Magnolias are one of your trademark flowers; what's the best way to cut them from a tree?

Louesa Use the general pruning rule and cut branches where they connect to the main branch. You should always cut where there is connectivity. Once cut, make another cut up into the wood end. This helps marginally, as it's not a flower but a blooming tree, and the water helps keep it hydrated and alive. I like to make a cross with two cuts in the wood.

Sarah How do you like to cut magnolia for small use in vessels?

Louesa Again, err on the side of cutting too tall; you can never add back the branch you cut. Then, place in a vessel with other flora and feel into it. The magnolia should steal the show always.

Sarah How long will magnolia last once cut?

Louesa They can last as long as two to even three weeks and force beautifully inside especially with heat, but there are so many variables from where they are placed in the house to the bloom itself. When you cut them as a bud they will open up beautifully inside, but if you bring in branches with existing blooms they will only last a couple of days, but then, in the case of the grandiflora, they turn a leathery burnished color that I love.

Sarah What's the best way to transport them?

Louesa Lay the magnolia flat in a vehicle with the bloom up. I like to make a pillow—in this case I used the passion flower underneath. Make sure you don't put anything on the blooms, as the perfect petals will break and bruise and brown.

Sarah I like the way you mix magnolia in their different stages of bloom. Is there anything you look for in shape?

Louesa Unlike a flower market, where everything is cultivated and uniform in size, when you forage you can get flowers budding and decaying on branches in all different stages of nature, which means you can mix tight with open and mangled blooms. Sometimes I take off three petals and just keep two. It's all about the mix and variety, but I do prefer odd numbers.

Sarah Vines can get really knotty and intertwined. What's the best way to forage them?

Louesa Passion flower is like any vine such as jasmine or clematis. You have to lift the vines off the ground or anything they are growing on, pull gently, and then cut them. I like to try and get as much length as possible. This is really a two-person job, with one person holding the end with the blossoms so they don't get damaged and the other person wrangling and cutting. The best is when you can cut it like a curtain so it comes off in one big piece, but then you still need to separate the vines, which is very labor-intensive and delicate work.

Sarah What about the fruit on the passion vines?

Louesa The riper the fruit, the more likely it will fall off. The green ones stay on more easily; this is true of almost all fruiting branches and vines.

Sarah Once cut, do you put the vines straight in water?

Louesa Put as much of the stem as possible in a bucket of water. It can be hard to get the right part of the stem in the water—you often need to work out which end is which. There can be five vines intertwined with heads at different ends. Luckily it can live long out of water and doesn't die easily at all. When you keep it in water it can keep on blooming for as long as two weeks. They are also really easy to propagate.

IN THE CEMETERY BEHIND MISSION DOLORES

Matthew has worked for me and more recently alongside me in every incarnation of my creative work life for the past decade—since he was a puppy at twenty. He has become family and the most true protégé I could hope for, often surpassing me in his work with his fairie ways.

Behind the Mission Dolores in San Francisco there is an alleyway with a fence completely draped with the most beautiful and fragrant white passion flower vines. The vines grow out of the Mission's old cemetery, which for a long time has been one of my favorite places to take shelter from the city. There are only three cemeteries left in San Francisco, the others having been transported to Colma at the beginning of the 20th century. The Mission Dolores Cemetery is the oldest, dating back to when the Mission was founded in 1776. Among the slightly decrepit white marble graves are old rose bushes and scented geraniums. Citrus, fig, and apple trees planted in the mid-1800s provide a canopy that lends the whole scene a remarkable filtered green light. It's the most perfect scenery. The passion flower vines grow up along the southern adobe wall and have taken over the chain link fences that enclose the paved schoolyard behind the Mission. Once this schoolyard was another part of the cemetery where about 5,000 Coastal Miwok and Ohlone Native Americans were buried.

I first discovered the passion flower vines a few years ago, on a date when I scaled the 30-foot fence and stole into the cemetery on the night of an eclipse. All the passion flowers were blooming and filled the air with their curious scent. It was a lovely surprise, as the Mission usually smells anything but nice. Like their fellow cemetery dwellers, these vines are of an older variety not so commonly seen. *Passiflora caerulea* or Constance Elliot was bred in the early 19th century and is noted for its hardiness, white blooms, and surprisingly strong fragrance. Finding that they hold up better than a lot of other passion flower vines, I began using them in my work with Louesa. I've discovered that they will continue to bloom weeks after they've been cut and, even more wondrous, will begin to root, not unlike nasturtiums. I've now propagated these cemetery passion flower vines a few times over.

Matthew Drewry Baker

Passion Fruit
Breakfast Bowl

from Heidi Swanson

I love this with the sweet coconut nectar swirl, but maple syrup or honey are both fine substitutes.

Makes one bowl. Double or triple the recipe based on the number of people you are serving.

1 cup plain, unsweetened Greek yogurt

Pulp and juice from ½ passion fruit

¾ tablespoon coconut nectar, maple syrup, or honey, or to taste

Pinch of fine grain sea salt

4 or 5 lightly smashed blackberries, or other seasonal berry

2 tablespoons toasted coconut flakes

2 tablespoons toasted almond slices

Dusting of bee pollen (optional)

Arrange the yogurt in a shallow bowl. Dollop the passion fruit on top of the yogurt, then drizzle with syrup. Use a spoon to gently swirl the syrup and passion fruit into the yogurt just a bit. Season with a hint of salt, before adding the berries. Sprinkle with coconut flakes, almond slices, and bee pollen.

I recommend herbs for you

don't go forgetting them in your rush from city to city

In your pants' pockets I put incense

and cicadas

and seaweed

Be sure they help you unravel the roads

I filled your eyes with crystal skylights and fishes

of silver and gold

just in case the light, in case the snails

in case again the night

into your ears I slipped sweet flutes

seven steps to heaven

with rocks and stones and trees to follow

the filters to wear on the chest

the unremitting voice of the nightly streams

then the circles of the zodiac

the rabbits with their daily ration of carrots

the white swallows

everything there is light

where light and shade repose

Conversation In Front of A Helicopter—Rosario Murillo

WINTER SOLSTICE

DECEMBER

Who has known the ocean? Neither you or I, with our
earth-bound senses, know the foam and surge of the tide
that beats over the crab hiding under the seaweed of
his tide pool home; or the lilt of the long, slow swells of
mid-ocean, where shoals of wandering fish prey and are
preyed upon, and the dolphin breaks the waves to breathe
the upper atmosphere.

Lost Woods: The Discovered Writing of Rachel Carson —Rachel Carson

bay · magnolia · cardoons · toyon
usnea lichen · clematis · tree dahlia
hydrangea · smokebush

Although we were well into year three of one of the worst droughts on record in modern California history, this did not preclude the occasional storm hammering its way down the West Coast and pummeling us with much-needed rain. When we started loading in to Saltwater, the Inverness restaurant of aquaculturist Luc Chamberlain, we were mid-storm, and the wind was driving the rain horizontally as it whipped across Tomales Bay. Outside in the parking lot bundles of bay branches stacked pile-high were taking a lashing, their green leaves glistening as they soaked up the rain.

Saltwater overlooks Tomales Bay in the small town of Inverness with the rolling hills of Marshall visible in the distance across the water. Between the two lies the San Andreas Fault, a silent reminder of bigger natural forces at play. The town, which first served as a weekend resort for city dwellers of San Francisco and Oakland over a century ago, still retains the charm of a weekend bolt-hole with some of the original small cottages still in use. Nestled under a ridge with its back to the Pacific, most of Inverness is hidden among the trees, with an air of dampness ever present, even in the driest of years. Climb the ridge and the view opens up to expanding vistas of Tomales Bay on one side and then on the other, Point Reyes National Seashore, an 80-mile expanse of unspoiled cliffs and sandy beaches.

The winter solstice was approaching, and the day was short and the light gloomy. The lights on the porch at Saltwater served as a warm beacon as we set up inside Luc's simple all-white, wood-clad restaurant, sipping cups of tea, the bay transforming the room into a druid's lair, our tribute to the solstice.

Sarah

of the earth able to host a large, varied and healthy lichen population (more than eighteen species). I am very glad for this. In my hikes and my working life I gravitate toward a few species—*Ramalina menziesii* (lace lichen), *Alectorias* (witch's hair) and *Usnea* lichen, most often seen on my beloved bay, oak, and Douglas fir trees.

Usnea longissima (old man's beard) is the longest lichen in the world, an uncommon and gracefully beautiful species. This extraordinary lichen grows in scattered spots in northern coastal ranges, often near a water source. It hangs, drapes, and falls from the trees, and in big winter storms can carpet the forest floor under those trees. It was the original Christmas tree tinsel, used for that purpose in Scandinavia and Northern Europe, but sadly rare in that part of the world due to air pollution.

For me it epitomizes a druid solstice, the progression from pantheistic traditions to Christmas today. The magical dark wet green forest, draped with living silver-gray lichen, the same magical gifts from the trees.

I forage only the lichen that has been blown or dropped to the forest floor. It would be ecologically wrong to pull any lichen from the trees, and this is a rule that should never be broken, especially given the fragile state of the ecosystems.

I wanted the vessels used for the installation to look and feel of the shore, and the dark damp green canopy of Inverness. One truism—if you source close to the nexus of your event, your chances of the flora, food, ceramics, textiles, etc. feeling organic and of that place are vastly higher.

The Sunday before the shoot, I stumbled upon Molly Prier's elfin

Bringing the wet, vibrantly green winter rainforest into a restaurant requires a thoughtful balance of too much, too wild, too wooly, an almost invisible human hand that cuts down the scale, prunes and places.

In addition, we cut 2-3 carloads of the tallest bay branches we could fit in our wagon. To achieve the installation goal of bringing the solstice forest into the restaurant, we made 3 trips totally full of our cuttings. Toyon, bay, fallen oak, and *Usnea* lichen along with a few prized blooms.

Most lichens are intolerant of air pollution, and we are very fortunate in West Marin to live in one of the few remaining semipopulated corners

ceramics compound during a West Marin open studio weekend. I'm not sure why or how we walked into that open studio, except we needed ceramics and I had a hunch. Molly inhabits quite possible the most romantic, diminutive, and perfectly magical cluster of tiny buildings not more than a crow's mile from Saltwater. It was rainy again and a short cold winter day, and her studio was an aromatic and warm refuge. She served spiced mulled cider in paper cups, and I begged her permission to borrow a few pieces for Luc's shoot. She happily offered, mostly due to goodwill toward Luc and June McCroy.

Her vessels look like shell; oysters and mussels, slightly moody, brooding and dark. Yet they possess a luminosity that I guess comes from Molly's lightness and happiness to be an artist living on the shores of Tomales Bay. She crafts what she sees, and they were seamless amongst all the wet bay and bloody magnolias. They almost disappeared, looking like stony creatures in the green winter landscape we attempted to recreate. And that made me happy and thankful.

As we were cutting the pristine bay in Inverness we came across a sweet warm woman with her elderly dachshund, who could not have been more welcoming. She talked about the moving experience of coming to California, this new world, from the Midwest as a child. It was something that resonated very strongly and was deeply personal to me. She triggered the memory for me of discovering a powerfully expansive, exotic landscape—so vastly different from Ohio, or Illinois, or my childhood Kentucky. She expressed the transformation that can take place at any age—for her as a young child, for me as a newly married woman in my early thirties.

She knew in her bones, as I did, that for many of us, once we came to visit, it was only a matter of time before we made Northern California our home. She was a kindred spirit, in that Tomales Bay and the gentle hills, forest, and grasslands around that body of water called her home. I remembered staying on the banks of Tomales Bay fifteen years ago . . . more, maybe . . . and knowing I was changed, in love really. So romantic is the landscape.

It's easy for a dining room table covered in bay branches to become imposing and messy. It is also easy to over-manicure and arrange, which to me is far worse and defeats the purpose of foraging.

One helpful approach is to place yourself at each place setting, and the heads of the table, working in circles around the table, over and over again. Where is the intersection between wild and sexy and tamed and approachable? If you look from every angle enough times, the answers should leap out at you.

In the winter I feel a need to bring aromatic branches into the house, then just a smattering of blooms, just like you see outdoors in California. A bloom is a more treasured find, like an orange used to be a treasured gift in the winter months, exotic and nourishing. Too many blooms at a holiday table intrinsically look purchased, because they most probably *are* purchased, imported from another part of the world. It is much more honest to include and even show off those few rare magnolia blooms, or the white camellias unblemished by the rain. They are a source of joy amongst all that green. That is how I feel when I find them in December, and that is how I want my guests to feel too.

Louesa

Sarah One of my favorite materials is the bay laurel, and it was the first material you and I ever worked with together, along with the fennel. What is the appeal for you?

Louesa Bay is one of my favorite trees. It's symbiotic with the oak and landscape here in West Marin and looks beautiful all year long. Even in the drought it looks OK; it's beautifully aromatic and has been used forever. The Native Americans ate the berries and it has many medicinal uses. California bay is much stronger than the European bay laurel, so you can't consume too much, as it can be slightly toxic. If you squeeze a bunch of the leaves in your hand it can give you a head rush.

Sarah How is it to work with?

Louesa It's so brilliant and easy to work with, with very sturdy branches, and it stacks beautifully. All the leaves grow in the same direction, and it's light. I can load up tons in my wagon because it all goes in the same direction. It's like fennel that way. You can work with gobs of it, and it's easy to cut and handle. When we did a 40-foot installation at Heath Ceramics, I foraged, cut, and transported it by myself. If you do it carefully you can keep packing it in.

Sarah I like the fact that you barely used any props to help install the bay

Louesa The less intervention and manipulation the better. I do have my twines of choice, but we had to tie only one branch for this shoot. Everything else was placed jenga-style relying on gravity to hold it in place. I used the structure of the branch to attach it to the beams and other branches.

Sarah You never worry about things falling?

Louesa People are so fearful of things falling that they tend to over-engineer things. When they hang paintings in their house maybe a nail would suffice. The same applies with installation work. People tend to over-tie things and make them more secure than needed.

Sarah What got you inspired to work with the sea elements?

Louesa Saltwater is more than a restaurant. It's a way of seeing things in its entirety. Luc is an oyster man who works with watershed issues. We're so land-based as a people that we don't think much of the sea. The earth is made up of more water than land, but it's strange that most people don't have a connection to that. Saltwater is Luc's manifestation of his relationship to the water around him.

Sarah What were you envisioning?

Louesa What we did with that installation is not food styling, it's about Luc and his connection to the oysters. I wanted it to be very primal —an underwater tableau. I wanted it to feel as close to what I find beautiful when I walk down to the shore—the inter-coastal land where the ocean and the earth meet. I wanted to articulate that beauty and composition in an elemental way.

Sarah We weren't into a traditional Christmas look, but we came up with a medieval/druid like table for the solstice.

Louesa The history of the Christmas tree comes from bringing in green at the darkest time of the year, but we have this very bright electric version. The Scandinavians with candles are more druid based. Bay lends itself to a variety of scales, and one big bunch can have big impact. You don't need to work with a fifty-foot installation of bay but can hang little wreaths or garlands. The smokebush is very spooky. I cut big branches, then cut it down for the table. It has a smoky whispiness to it that makes it very moody. We recycled the cardoons from another shoot. I prefer them to artichoke blossoms as they have a very soft, fibrous quality and they're golden, soft and spikey and feathery. Then the magnolias in bloody-burgundy red made it very holiday.

THE LEANEST MONTH

JANUARY

Of all the possibilities considered, the capacity to experience beauty seemed like one of the best reasons for living. Beauty is an involuntary response to a high-order pattern recognition. Perhaps it is even a glimpse into our mind's underlying perceptual architecture. As such, beauty is a kind of "enlightenment" that reveals something fundamental about the way in which the world appears to us.

Wabi-Sabi: Further Thoughts —Leonard Koren

passion flower • date palms
solandra • cobaea • jasmine

"We don't have enough" was a frequent refrain from Louesa, and it had set off alarm bells when I heard her say it on our very first shoot, even though there were gobs of fennel piled high and the longest leeks I had ever seen. It took me a few shoots to realize that no matter how much we had, Louesa always knew there was more to be had out there. So when I heard her lament the lack of materials as we began setting up at the Venice loft of noted art director Tamotsu Yagi, I was unperturbed— until, that is, I saw everything laid out in the tiny back yard. Indeed, it was paltry pickings.

Los Angeles has always been a notoriously difficult place to forage, in Louesa's book. The great concrete urban expanse with its freeways has very little abandoned green space. Chuck in the epic drought and the time of year—January is difficult to forage in most places—and it was looking decidedly bleak. In fact, we had chosen Yagi's loft as our January location as we knew the simple, streamlined, minimal look of his studio-cum-home would work well with only a few simple floral elements, the restraint and austerity of the design in his outstanding collection of pieces by Jean Prouvé and Charlotte Perriand allowing the flora to stand alone. Juxtaposed with the furnishings are shelves filled with Yagi's collectables: a veritable mix of Darwin-meets-Duchamp finds ranging from seed pods and a bird's nest to botanical specimens in jars, with the occasional ceramic object and piece of conceptual art. It was against this backdrop, with the sun low in the sky casting weak shadows across the room, that we shot the spartan foraged finds of January.

Sarah

The sprawl of Los Angeles is full of contradictions. The vastness of roads and concrete can feel deceptively full of the promise of plentiful specimens, but often sadly translates into countless hours of wasted time in the car looking for a few choice branches and blooms.

When I work in the Bay Area my mind is full of conscious and unconscious maps . . . years of driving nearly every road in Oakland, Berkeley, and San Francisco and many in Sonoma have created a web of knowledge—what's happening, growing, thriving in every month. What I look for, what's easily accessible, what's abundant, what needs pruning. After about two years of traveling the roads this way in LA I guess I have accumulated a fair amount of physical memory and knowledge. I don't write much of this mapping information down; I welcome the opportunity to use my mind this way, without notes.

Whenever I work in LA, I experience a bipolar sort of journey. I honestly love the wacky surreal landscape that couldn't be more different than the northern part of the state, hypersaturated with its cartoonish California-ness! It's fertile to me in its lack of rules and dogma, and even in its ugliness. I also gain more and more thankfulness for the lush, abundant garden of Eden of Northern California.

The drought has compounded the scarcity of flora to be found in LA and has increased the time I need to spend sourcing.

I know that nearly everything I forage, glean, source, or use is alive only due to human intervention. I also know the landscape bears no likeness to what it looked like before over 100 years of ill-planned water and land "management." When you drive to Palm Springs, due east, you quickly see what LA would look like without water.

So this year we mostly found drought-tolerant southern hemisphere flora; cobaea, solandra, dates, and an outlier, jasmine. I didn't want to use blooms thriving due to a human hand.

Solandra, informally referenced as the chalice vine, has become one of my most sought-after treasures. I first discovered them in LA and now we are growing them in Stinson Beach. They are powdery, golden, poisonous, Arthurian cups full of pollen and scent and mystery.

January in LA would be spartan and lean in any year. This year was amplified.

Louesa

How the flowering date palm came to rest on Yagi's Lucite pillar was an impromptu moment of pure collaboration.

This neon Lucite piece became a mirror, a representation of so much that of my visual experience of LA. Postmodern objects, 1970s neon—pop colors, Ed Ruscha color stories, geometric lines, more male than female, garish neon signs. Artificial light layered on glaring California sun. A calm pillar of color, bouncing pale shadows of acid green around the room . . . and fracturing any natural curvature of flora.

It became an unexpected moment of psychedelia that was utterly fitting and, I think, stunning.

Contrast is compelling. The table covered in pale pink butcher paper became a restrained study of contrasts.

Informed by Yagi's industrial space, I decided to bring some of my pharmaceutical glass I knew would be at home there.

The spare "floral" elements composed on a sprawling table with lots of glass, filled with lots of water and lit by the harsh winter sun, created the desired effect. Water . . . water became a primary element of beauty, defining the glass and the flora . . . and holding light. Not much water to be found in the outdoor landscape, but water illuminated each vessel, bouncing light all around the room. One of the solandra blooms that didn't survive my cutting and transport became a sea creature, submerged in Yagi's doughnut glass vessel . . . a second life.

Although we occasionally brought in some of our own vessels for the shoots, we mostly relied on what was at hand, working with the design elements of the space. When Yagi saw Louesa wrangling a date palm, he quietly disappeared, returning with a Lucite table leg designed by his one-time friend, noted Japanese designer Shiro Kuramata. He placed the neon green and pink leg upon the table to serve as a pedestal for the date palm, with the effect of completely transforming its form and the pinkish fronds picking up the neon hues of the Lucite.

Sarah Where do you typically forage in LA?

Louesa I look for industrial wastelands and abandoned lots. I've looked at friends' gardens, but everything is much more manicured in LA, and I've found very few interesting ones. Koreatown is less gentrified; there are a lot of empty lots. I've found passion vine on chain link fences, also solandra or chalice vine. Weedy, viny flora grow well. There's nothing in Brentwood or Santa Monica, but I've found fennel and nasturtium in Santa Monica Canyon. Venice has some decent alleys. I've had no luck with the hills, like Echo Park. Too many parts of town have so much freeway pollution.

Sarah Do you always feel pressure to deliver?

Louesa Think of fishing: you never say, "Go and catch six salmon in six hours." You fish and see what you catch. It's a lot of pressure to do an event with 100-percent gleaned materials. For a dinner party or a wedding I'll often call on other resources, like a friend's garden, or work with farmers or a grower if I know I can't forage everything in time.

Sarah For this shoot we had planned on working with few materials.

Louesa We knew not to bring masses of stuff. What I bring is greatly informed by the person I am working with. It's a dialogue between that person, their work, and their space. I wanted it to be spare. We decided no roses. It's a masculine space with hard surfaces; roses would have looked weird.

Sarah The date palms proved a great resource.

Louesa People go crazy for them, and I can always find them in LA. There are over forty different types. I cut the entire stalk, which contains the often edible date fruit. Most of these fruiting date palms are female, with varied colors: dusty pink, pale lavender, gray, ink blue, and every shade of orange. They looked very sea creature–like, almost like an anemone—powerful objects that drew people in. From retail work I know anything that feels or looks like an undersea creature, like an octopus or squid, is visually powerful.

Sarah How do you forage the date palms?

Louesa I found them for the first time in an alley in Venice and now I am primed to see them. I'll remember where these were and come back and cut them. It's like when you are in love and you have a song, suddenly you hear that song everywhere. You're primed to hear it. It's the same with mapping flora.

Sarah I've become used to your working with mass. Here you managed to create something beautiful with very little.

Louesa This shoot was more sculptural and spare, all about negative space. No volume—more of a suggestion. It's the antithesis of working with mass, as you can see each bloom and tendril and you also really see the vessels. The light and vessels become a much stronger element with less. If we had a lot of materials we would never have created that cool convergence with Tamotsu bringing out the table leg. It was a sweet collaboration, his viewpoint coming together with the flora.

RINTARO

FEBRUARY

The relentless complexity of the world is off to the side of the trail. For hunters and herders trails weren't always so useful. For a forager, the path is *not* where you walk for long. Wild herbs, camas bulbs, quail, dye plants, are away from the path. The whole range of items that fulfill our needs is out there. We must wander through it to learn and memorize the field—rolling, crinkled, eroded, gullied, ridged (wrinkled like the brain)—holding the map in mind. For the forager, the beaten path shows nothing new, and one may come home empty-handed.

The Practice of The Wild—Gary Snyder

nasturtium · magnolia campbellii
magnolia x soulangeana · magnolia liliiflora
magnolia denudata · willow · buckeye

We had been looking forward to shooting at Rintaro, Sylvan Mishima Brackett's izakaya, in San Francisco's Inner Mission District and quite possibly the most beautiful Japanese restaurant in the nation. The Chez Panisse alum had conceived of the restaurant over a decade ago, and its making is very much a family affair and a labor of love, the simple food inspired by Sylvan's Japanese mother's home cooking as well as from his annual summer trips back to Japan where Sylvan would watch his grandmother cook. The traditional handcrafted wood interiors are the work of his father, Len Brackett, a full-fledged temple carpenter who apprenticed in Kyoto.

Louesa has been doing the flora at Rintaro ever since its opening in fall 2014, and although it was February, this being California, the first signs of spring were already happening with the green leaves of the buckeye just breaking open, offering a portent of what was to come. It seemed only fitting that the hyper-natural environment of Rintaro, with its salvaged unfinished woods and soil-plastered walls, should have the freshest, wildest flora.

Sarah

Rintaro is a place that holds great meaning for me, a place that I consider one of my homes. I cannot be remotely objective, nor can I think of it as a "restaurant." It's even a bit odd for me to realize that for some people it's just exactly that, an unusually beautifully crafted restaurant.

Sylvan Mishima Brackett and I came from the same family tree that so many in our little spot of earth grew up in, Chez Panisse. Our tenures there didn't officially overlap, but it's a big web that connects us.

Sylvan is one of the very few people I've ever known whose aesthetic I consider to be flawless. Every choice, ever gesture, every small and large detail of his business is perfect to me.

When I lost my business in the economic crash of 2008–2009 many friends and colleagues from the Chez Panisse family came forth to offer me work. One of the sweet things in life is the surprise of who offers support and loyalty when life is hard. Sylvan was one of those people, who quickly absorbed me into his new and slightly gonzo catering company, Peko-Peko.

I was so broke and so unmoored that I agreed to any and all work with Sylvan's crew, and the hard work and sense of camaraderie was very good medicine. Most gigs I would forage and glean, install small to huge elaborate flora, stay and run the front of the house, and often I stayed late into the night washing dishes and packing the car. It was incredibly good for my mind and my body and I learned a lot from the Japanese work ethic of "working yourself to death."

Sylvan respected and understood my work, and this gave me a great deal of energy and will to keep creating and building my new trade even when it paid very little. Needless to say, those years fostered a great deal of loyalty and kinship between us and the ragtag crew of Peko Peko and then what became Rintaro.

Rintaro is the only restaurant where we do weekly floral installations. Help from Matthew Drewry Baker and my partner, Curtis, make this possible; I could not do it on my own. Sylvan and I operate on a barter basis: flowers for the best Japanese izakaya food in America seems like a good trade.

The space—warm wood, temple interior—is the perfect foil for the minimal but lush new spring nasturtium and buttery magnolias arriving in Feburary. This interior looks stunning with both minimal, bare and sculptural flora, or with lush, layered, verdant floral. We have learned it's not a great backdrop for bright garish colors—I think it's too intelligent and warm wood for that.

I try and avoid clichés, but I guess nasturtium and magnolias are quintessentially Japanese. Here is another area where Sylvan and I overlap. We both consciously and unconsciously marry old-world Japan and new world Northern California in our work. I like to think it comes naturally.

For this shoot I just looked literally at what was in my yard and my Stinson Beach neighborhood and roadsides. I find the vibrant, water filled, deep deep green nasturtium of California late winter early spring endlessly beautiful and poetic. Many consider them a "weed." What a tremendous misnomer that is. Not only are they lovely, but every part of them is edible and delicious. In fact, we often bring Rintaro nasturtium buds to adorn savory dishes and pastry. They bloom almost all year with enough water, December to July at least. They seem to contain the most life force in the winter and early spring with cool plentiful rains and full creeks. They create wonderful arrangements as single vines or massed as you see them here. You have to let nasturtium leaves bend and reach in the same direction they were growing. They are tenacious and tender plants, and I can't see any logical reason to force them into new positions. They follow the sun and light. So much of this work is simply listening to what the plant is so obviously telling us, rather than imposing or interfering. This is a very clear example to me of hearing a song, a cadence, and a refrain in the movement of the leaves.

The magnolias articulate a very different rhythm. For one, they are a branch, not a vine, and they can't be bent or forced into positions; they can only be placed. The idea of the soft buttery sweetly expressive nasturtium paired with dramatic and woody magnolia appeals to me. They inhabit different worlds, one firmly on the ground and one seen mostly against the sky.

Pale yellow magnolias, commonly called yellow lantern, are rare and slow growing and blooming. Most people with a tree are hesitant to share the exquisite blooms. My old friend Nancy Olin generously offered the tree up the street, in its peak of blooming. These blooms are even more delicate and difficult to transport. They show bruising and break quite easily, and we exercised even greater caution loading them in with the buckets of nasturtium from our yard.

Magnolias are unabashedly my one true love amongst all blooms . . . well, there may be another lover or two.

Louesa

SO MUCH OF THIS WORK IS SIMPLY LISTENING TO WHAT THE PLANT IS SO OBVIOUSLY TELLING US, RATHER THAN IMPOSING OR INTERFERING.

Magnolias will grow from seed, cuttings, or grafts, and date back at least 144 million years in North America. They predate bee pollination and were initially pollinated by beetles.

They are also perfection in Rintaro. We use them nearly all year long; how lucky we are in Northern California. If there is a magnolia of any variety blooming in San Francisco, Oakland, Marin, or Sonoma, we will find it.

Many years ago I saw photos of a then avant-garde floral stylist from London. At the time I had no notion or interest in ever making this my vocation, but as an artist I was struck by what seemed a radical idea of arranging the entire plant, mostly of one kind, so that they tilted and bent in the same curved direction. It made a big impression on me, and I spent a fair amount of time thinking *why don't more florists do this?* It seemed so obvious, and so true. This was what I pictured when we arranged the large squat vessel on the bar at Rintaro for this shoot. I wanted all of the nasturtium to lean longingly in one direction, as if searching for the sun or blown by the wind. One of the masses we had cut by the creek that morning in Stinson Beach did just that. Again we just needed to gently position, secure them through balance and trickery, and let them be. Once the nasturtium were in position I could add the buttery magnolias—I imagined them as the tree under which the nasturtium grows.

My favorite magnolia is *Magnolia campbelli*, a mountain species from the kingdoms of Sikkim and Bhutan. Huge flowers the size of a child's head, creamy white or pale, clear pink. Borne on the end of a leafless branch, they have an unusual cup-and-saucer shape, and an Alice in Wonderland distorted size. They seem carnival or cartoony to me. The unusual cup-and-saucer shape is due to the inner petals being held erect in a cone at the reproductive parts. Trees seldom flower until they are more than twenty years old. Sadly the wood has long been used for tea boxes in China, so it is not a common sight anymore to see these trees in bloom on the mountains.

Louesa

Sarah We ended up using nasturtium, magnolia, and willow. Was that what you had in mind?

Louesa Typically February is a really beautiful month on the coast, as it is starting to be spring and things can be quite lush and vibrantly green, a psychedelic/acid trip green. It's one of my favorite months, as having the beginning of spring in February feels like this crazy luxury when you are not from here. This winter, however, was different because of the drought and the unusual weather patterns that made it colder and darker later in the winter. I just looked at what was happening in my immediate environment and that was nasturtium. The longer I do this work the more I fall in love with them.

Sarah What is it about them?

Louesa They are charmingly beautiful and you can see all their veins in the leaves. They are very tenacious and invasive and some people consider them a weed, but they're also the definition of tender. The leaves crush and bruise so easily yet they are tough and tenacious—I like the dichotomy.

Sarah I like the way you used them en masse at Rintaro.

Louesa People typically use them in dorky farmhouse-style little arrangements, but when you put them with farm flowers you don't see the beauty of the nasturtium. They should be completely on their own or minimally with one other flower.

Sarah How did you get the mass?

Louesa We used the nasturtium from the garden for the small arrangements but also went down to the creek beds in town and cut some in order to create the mass. We looked for nasturtium that were big and leggy and developed—not the delicate garden ones.

Sarah You described them as "quintessentially ikebana."

Louesa It's my Northern California take on what I find compositionally compelling about Japanese flower arranging. I like the single long tendril that can be so sculptural and poetic. We cut a nastursium tendril from the yard, and it grew a foot toward the light in the bedroom in just a few days—they are meant to propagate and spread. They can last for about two weeks indoors and come in a wide variety of shades, from creamy salmon, bright orange, and pale yellow to deep empress red.

Sarah Do you discuss with Sylvan what you are going to do?

Louesa No, but it's a very symbiotic relationship, as it's a place where hyper seasonality is integral to the work—that's what Sylvan's food is about and it's the same with the flora.

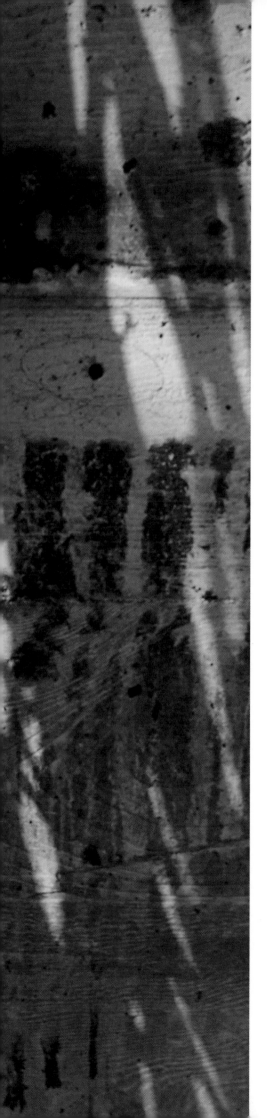

Sarah What is different about creating an installation in a restaurant as opposed to a home? Since this is ongoing, what do you have to keep in mind?

Louesa The ongoing nature of the work is positive. The more you work in a space, the more you have an understanding of the spatial relations, what works where, what shades of wood need to be considered, how the lighting is in different spots, and what the moods of the various areas of the restaurant are. The more you have an understanding of and relationship with the space, the more beautiful and easier the work becomes. It also helps that I already have a relationship with Sylvan and know his aesthetics and preferences.

Sarah What's the downside of a restaurant?

Louesa The physical environment of a restaurant is so singularly punishing, more than any other environment I work in. So much heat is coming off the kitchen, and Rintaro is an open kitchen. It's also very hot and stuffy from all the body heat of the people coming into the restaurant. Plants are really sensitive, and all that heat puts them in a state of distress. My work with foraged materials is especially ill suited for a restaurant, so it's challenging to find out what works. It also means that we have to go in two to three times a week and also rely on help from the restaurant to make sure the water is maintained—flowers consume a huge amount of water, especially in a restaurant. There's a reason people tend to use branches, succulents, and orchids that require only weekly maintenance.

Sarah What have you discovered working in this space over time?

Louesa We quickly discovered that the room at the back of the restaurant is a completely different ecosystem and we can create arrangements that are more conventionally romantic and brambly and horizontal. The little shelves lend themselves to tendrily-viny things that dangle down. I don't like pink in the front of the restaurant—except for magnolia—but in the back it's more moody so I can do a lot of bright colors in a more abstract way.

Sarah What works in the front?

Louesa Vertical, sculptural arrangements. The front has much more natural light with soaring ceilings so, height works here. I can bring in branches ten to sixteen feet tall and they look good at the bar. Here I used tall willow branches, one of my favorite plants with magnolia. It's really long and graceful but it's also flexible and it adds tremendous height and drama without being a big heavy branch. I have an important relationship with willow, as it lines the roads driving to and from Stinson to SF. It grows everywhere and beautifully in West Marin and there are many varieties of willow all along the stream beds. We used the creek dogwood, which is vibrant red and/or orange depending on the time of year, as it adds saturated color and pairs well with magnolia. There are not many other branches that I like to pair with magnolia.

IDES OF MARCH

MARCH

I have said to the worm: Thou art my mother
and my sister.

The Complete Illuminated Works — William Blake

wisteria · roses · lilac · apple blossoms
redbud · jasmine · forget-me-nots

Nothing can really prepare you for a visit to David Lee Hoffman's home and tea business (The Phoenix Collection) in Lagunitas. Drive up a winding hill behind the local store in this small, unincorporated Marin town and all of a sudden you know you have arrived at the Hoffman residence when the modest wooden homes amid the canopies of trees give way to what appears to be a small Chinese village stacked on the hillside. It's a sight to behold—in total twenty-five hand-built structures connected by narrow alleys and stairs join the different levels on the property, much of which sits almost suspended in the trees.

The "Last Resort," as David has dubbed his home, has been his life's work for the past forty years. He has created his own environmentally sustaining ecosystem that tackles waste management, water reuse, and food production using worm castings, composting, and graywater. David cleans his dishes with a mix of ash and shell; cooks entirely with wood, both indoors and out; and bakes bread with a solar oven. On the terraces leading up to the property are his organically composted gardens with vegetable and fruit that he harvests throughout the year.

Soil and terroir have come to define David Lee Hoffman and have put the tea pioneer on the map. The California-born native, now seventy, spent a decade in the sixties traveling throughout Asia, hanging out in China with rural tea farmers and Tibetan monks (where he got to know the Dalai Lama) and occasionally living with nomadic tribes where he drank pu-erhs and learned to appreciate the art of simple living.

On his return he was gradually drawn into the world of tea, encouraged by friends asking him to bring back some of his great tea finds from his travels. This was in the year 1990, and in Communist China tea was very much a corporate affair; use of chemicals and pesticides had become commonplace. David shunned the big businesses, opting for taste over volume and choosing to work directly with small farmers who avoided pesticides, an approach that befuddled the authorities. His low-key yet relentless pursuit of working directly with the individual tea farmer prevailed and ultimately succeeded in changing the face of tea in the States. David is considered to be a major influence in the growth of organic, handcrafted teas and is responsible for introducing flowering teas—bundles of tea leaves wrapped around blossoms—to this country. His work has also influenced the sales of tea in China, where markets now exist for the small individual tea farmer to sell directly to the consumer.

Share tea with David, and his passion is unrestrained as he pours a cup, smells the bouquet, then finally sips the tea, sucking it through his teeth, noting all the subtleties of flavor. Tea, like wine, pulls its flavor from the soil. A gentle, soft-spoken man, David showed nothing but equanimity in the knowledge that at any moment his hillside home could be razed. He has been in a lengthy, long-running dispute with Marin County officials over building permits for the Last Resort, which he never obtained. Although David is fully aware of his negligence, for him, creating a self-sustaining structure was a conscious choice to put the future of the earth ahead of the law.

Sarah

David's kitchen was a tiny space in the most comforting den-like manner. Everything you could see was burnished—the wood, the stoneware vessels, the dried fishes, the tea—every bit had a caramelized, almost tobacco patina, varnished. Even the antique linen tea towels used to wash the cups and plates with ash had become a deep, warm yet ashen gray, of the earth. A familiar sense of antiquity filled me. *Primitive* is a complicated and colonial word and loaded. *Ancient* sounds too academic or religious as a descriptive. Perhaps *rural* and *elemental*, a place difficult to define by any century seems close to describing my first impression of the Last Resort—well, the kitchen at least.

David served us shiitake mushrooms stuffed with proper breadcrumbs and aged Gouda, steeped in pu-erh of course. Rich and burnished also, deeply warming. The pu-erh tea on this first visit was extremely strong, an entirely different buzz from my steady and constant stream of green tea; in fact, the buzz lasted into the evening. Curtis and I both said how representative this was of the countless differences between Japanese and Chinese culture. Tiny tiny white porcelain cups of bracing tea, meant to keep you working and warm, with no languid naps.

All cooking was done over wood; heating also, if there was much heating in the rambling structures. David mostly sleeps outside. Sleeping outside, drinking massive amounts of tea, some wine. He will probably live forever because of it; a mantra I heard from everyone on the shoot.

These is no doubt to me that this intensely rich soil, pure air, and oxygenated water, peaceful bees, and the attentive hand of Martine (David's garden manager) produced the most pristine apple blossom branch I had ever found. With pink variegated blossoms, flawless white single petal blooms, and a sweet gentle nose.

It was so singular and such a gift that I couldn't bring myself to cut it. (Curtis and Martine did that for me.) I also couldn't bring myself to cut more than one branch, a good lesson for me.

Louesa

Every time I try to write about the foraging, gleaning, and arranging at the Last Resort I keep coming back to the place, with all the streams and eddies of stories. It feels compacted and condensed and at the same time expansive and full of hidden spaces yet to be discovered: Terry Gilliam meets rural 19th century preindustrial China, meets back-to-the-landers in Marin County circa 1972. The Last Resort still embodies that "alternative" universe, thank god. To me David has created a lifelong installation that embodies a belief system, and an oddly elegant aesthetic. Much like other folk art installations, such as the Watts Towers in LA or Arcosanti in Arizona. But we must come back to flowering spring branches and tiny dear forget-me-nots, heavenly scented lilac and jasmine, and always roses.

We spent two full days foraging in Marin, and more time gleaning on David's verdant, fertile acre. It was the height of "spring" in Marin, with all of the most beloved blossoming trees full of vibrant pinks, purple, and snowy white. We found bright healthy end-of-season redbud trees right in the Lagunitas valley, long meandering apricot David Austin roses hanging over a creek in Ross (next to the police station). We cut from hedges and hedges of pale yellow Lady Banks roses, also along a creek bed, near Marin General. We spotted white lilacs growing over a fence in an empty lot—well, really a construction zone—growing from an old bush in an also empty house. Very rare on every level, more rare and precious to me than peonies from New Zealand. And the "unusual" warm dry winter resulted in wisteria laden with early heavy blooms, big blooms I feared would be short lived.

Wandering around one of David's many industrial remnant lumber piles, being careful of snakes, I found a bed of tiny densely blue forget-me-nots. I love them so—not native, invasive, and totally perfect to me, blue, blue, blue. They can get wild and leggy, they last forever, they summon so many corny, sentimental meanings, and did I say blue?

According to German legend the forget-me-not (*Myosotis*, mouse ear) takes its name from the last words of a romantic knight who drowned while trying to pick a bouquet from the banks of a swiftly moving springtime river, for his lady.

Sarah This felt like one of the biggest gleanings to date, no?

Louesa I wouldn't say the biggest, but the most bountiful. There is something so intrinsically uplifting about spring blossoms because they are so fertile. Even though we don't have the extreme deprivation of winter here in California there is still a memory of winter darkness. Spring is very primal and joyful. Fall is equally rich and bountiful but has a different emotional quality.

Sarah The apple blossom was extraordinarily beautiful.

Louesa That was the most pristine and beautiful blossom, I think in great part owing to David's gardens and grounds being biodynamic, and his belief system that plants are sentient beings.

Sarah The redbud in particular was on fire.

Louesa Most people think of redbud as an Eastern plant; it's native in the Smoky Mountains and in the Eastern mountain ranges, and I grew up seeing it. It does better with a frost and doesn't do great in the Bay Area but there will be little pockets here and there. We found this on the roadside as we were driving up. I think it's phenomenal. It's like forsythia. It's the first bright powerful harbinger of spring.

Sarah The wisteria was perfect for this Asian-esque setting, but you say it's hard to forage?

Louesa Bees love it but most people don't. Wisteria and lilac and tuberose are a common allergen. I would have it in the store at Erica Tanov and people got headaches, itchy eyes, and asthma—it's pretty intense. It's so woody and dry and doesn't hydrate well, and it's nearly impossible to get hydration at the end. It's one reason why flower mart flowers tend to be stockier and not willowy. Wisteria is very fleeting, but it's beautiful when it dies and it makes a terrible mess, but I think it looks good with petals everywhere. Either you love that or you can't deal. If I'm being pragmatic, it's the perfect thing for a dinner party, a one-time use. It has the most beautiful drapey waterfall form. The combination of the wood structure with all the tendrils makes it poetic and romantic, and the color runs from deep purple to a pale, pale lilac that's almost white. The white is the more fragile—that's true with most white flowers.

Sarah How do you work with its weepy form?

Louesa It doesn't lend itself to most vessels, as it's very thick and the branches go in a million directions. You need a big vessel, but it's hard to use in big pieces. It's easier to use when you break it down into individual pieces or into a couple of sprigs. It's good to cut up that woodiness, which we did, and then placed in the teapots.

Sarah You love to work with scale, and this proved to be one of our best locations to showcase this.

Louesa David's place afforded us this incredible opportunity to use big branches focused on large scale with these extraordinary walls and surfaces and vessels both inside and out. It was like a movie set where we could do cinematic installations on a grand scale. It was very much a process of creating beauty in the moment. It felt like creating sand mandalas that are built, then swept away.

Sarah We also had a huge array of vessels to choose from.

Louesa I think David Hoffman's is a great example of working with an extraordinary collection of objects and vessels. It was my fantasy location where we just rummaged around and found incredible objects on site. There was endless stuff that was beautiful. Everywhere you looked there were vessels, objects, textures. It was the perfect combination of industrial salvage and handcrafted, hewn hippie pieces, that with of course a million cups and teapots.

Sarah I like the way you relied on the same components inside but created a very different look.

Louesa Inside was about coming in and having tea together. How would you take the same materials used outside at an industrial scale then break them down to an intimate human scale to make it beautiful, opulent, and romantic.

Sarah What's your thinking when you place all the teapots out on the table first in their little groupings?

Louesa For something small like this—or a dinner table—you begin by bringing all the vessels to the table first and filling them all with water. You put them in place so it's the beginning of a composition and you see how they are in dialogue with each other. I look at the movement with the vessels on the table that way when I arrange them; I can build so that it becomes one organism. I like to add elements and take away. I can't do that if I am bringing in one piece at a time like an assembly line.

Sarah I like the way you left out a couple of lids.

Louesa With the groupings I like to leave out an occasional single tea pot, or a few lids, or place a tea pot with the spout turning out —or maybe show a pretty handle. If you use people's pieces you can showcase their viewpoint and what they love. There should be threads of them throughout the work. And likewise, building even a tiny collection of vessels for your home can add so much beauty and individuality to your floral touches at home. Make it your own.

REALM OF THE SENSES

APRIL

There are things that are not sayable. That's why we have art.

¿El mundo que pinto? No sé si lo invento, yo creo que más bien es ese mundo el que me inventó a mi.

The Oval Lady—Leonora Carrington

peonies · roses
passion flower · poppies

Berkeley-based artist Lauren McIntosh is one of those rare individuals whose whole approach to living seems to embody the creation of beauty, whether it be through her dark yet colorful paintings; her revered store, Tail of the Yak, in Berkeley; or her work at Creative Growth, the Oakland art center that serves adult artists with developmental, mental, and physical disabilities; or simply through the things she chooses to surround herself with. It's inspiring to be around. She cuts a striking figure in an Alice-in-Wonderland-with-a-dash-of-Marie-Antoinette sort of way, and the Berkeley home that she shares with her husband, Stephen Walrod, a fellow patron of the arts, is a testament to all this. It was against a backdrop of marble tables, glass cloches, citrine Fortuny silk curtains, paintings, folk art, and a collection of extraordinary 19th-century European porcelain that we staged our April shoot. We began outdoors, wandering through her Californian take on a European-style garden, formal with just the right amount of wild. The colors on this day are subdued under a gray April sky, but we find plenty of roses and extraordinary creamy peony-like poppies with crepe-ish petals to accompany the buckets of peonies awaiting us inside, their choice inspired by Lauren's collection of delicately ornate porcelain vases.

Sarah

Lauren McIntosh is a dear friend. An artist with a historical ambiguousness, an ancient and polyglot spirit, a singular persona with a royal countenance. She is a kindred soul in her love of all critters and most flora. An idiosyncratic woman who is driven to create, and who embodies fierceness and fragility. I think most authentic artists have a complicated recipe of toughness, resiliency, youthful tenacity, curiosity, and courage . . . with a very large dose of fragility.

She has created a singular realm of luxury and lushness—no trendy minimalism here—a profusion of saturated color, with diverse, cultural and historical references. Wildly inspiring to most. I call it a Shakespearean acid trip, a pagan Mexican song, a surreal world of spirits and creatures dead and alive.

She showed us her new Germanic-English 1800s ornate porcelain collection. I immediately realized we must shoot her stepson's biodynamicaly grown peonies paired with this new obsessive collection. Her home contained all the anti-minimalism I craved for the book. A plan was hatched, only to come to fruition nearly a year later.

How many heads of peonies were waiting for us in the kitchen? Two hundred? Three hundred? Probably—but my mind stopped at the sight of all of them all. So uniform—the same sherbet color family, the same tightness, the same length, and a few frilly varieties. No curving lines, no wonky bends, no tendrils, no seedpods or dead bits or half-formed blooms. I wasn't sure what to do with the mass of opulent peonies.

As a friend said, all the work had been done for me already. Or at least the physical wrangling, the hunting, the transportation, the cutting down, and the series of decisions—the best part—the decisions. What do I cut, how long, what do I remove, how short, can it be broken down—you can't go back—then which vines are married to which flowers ? Who's dating, who is an unlikely pair? All of these thought processes and decisions had been taken away from me prematurely, in Oregon.

We had some of this gleaning process when we walked through Lauren's thoughtfully and classically designed and tended garden as a team. What would I cut that had a bit of wild, or a bit of a foil for the peonies? What was our color story going to be? How long, how big, how brambly could it be and still make sense with the peonies? What would enable this shoot to look and feel like my work and this book—and still be a representation of Lauren's fantastical world?

At some point in the day we all ended up in Lauren's steeple-like studio. It's a little like everyone ending up in the kitchen at a lively party; it always happens. It's only a question of when. Now that I sit here and try and recall . . . we migrated down the stairs, but it felt like we were going up into a light-filled chapel. We migrated there because Lauren was sitting, peacefully painting, amidst the usual clamor and lightly frenetic energy of a photo shoot. What a perfect coping mechanism for the slightly unnerving energy of a shoot in your home. I was slightly envious of her solitary distraction.

Louesa

THE ROSES, PEONIES, AND PIGMENTS SAY IT BETTER THAN I DO.

Who could ever describe the layers upon layers of pigments, ceramics, papers, ephemera, tools and brushes, easels and paintings completed and half finished that this studio possessed.

This room allowed me to open up, loosen up, take some of Lauren's saturated color into myself totally and create arrangements that broke away from the perfectly composed formality of the living and dining rooms and the peony blooms upstairs.

Here the peonies and the roses could become a touch more understated, breaking free of the 18th century and coming into 1970s California. Or Mexico in 1949 . . . or Portugal in 1920, that is what happens at Lauren's home: a wonderful disorientation of time and place feels correct.

Sarah This is the only place where we ever used materials that were bought and also not grown in state, albeit very close. Why this aberration?

Louesa This was an organic decision. Peonies were my original inspiration for this chapter, and they are singular in their lushness. Everyone loves peonies, and it just made sense with Lauren's aesthetic and the fact that her stepson runs a biodynamic farm in Oregon. We weren't buying from across the world but from someone in our community. You obviously can't forage peonies in California, since they don't grow well here, and out of state you can cut them from a garden, but it's not like they grow wild and can be foraged. There are a lot of choices when buying flowers, but I think you should make the best ecological decision you can. Avoid agribusiness and flowers flown in from across the world. Buy them locally from as sustainable a source as you can. Just be conscientious when you buy.

Sarah What is the difference in handling cultivated flowers rather than those you have foraged?

Louesa There is something so beautiful and lush about the sheer mass of peonies, but when I am confronted with a sense of uniformity, what makes it interesting to me is to bring in elements that feel less cultivated. We walked the garden with Lauren and I looked for a foil, something with a different sense of line and less pristine but that still has a dialogue with the peonies. It still has to be in the same narrative. Mostly I wanted something with a different scale but in the same color palette.

Sarah When you work with extraordinary vessels, how much do they come into play? What dictates the composition—flora or vessels?

Louesa When I conceptualized this shoot I had this porcelain collection in mind, but the flora is just as important as the vessel. It's not one or the other, it's all one song. It's one aesthetic and they are in dialogue. You have to treat all your materials with respect and the way you handle them is vital. You can't have anything in your work that is ugly, plastic, or faux, not of the same integrity and the same aesthetic vocabulary as the flora. It all breaks down with bad vessels.

Sarah With these vases what was your thinking with placement?

Louesa Never evens; it's too uniform and symmetrical. I like to create clusters of negative space or clusters of density. I'll treat three arrangements as one, or two as one, or five as two, then add a tiny addition to the side that talks to the bigger one.

Sarah You've referred to arranging as a form of synesthesia?

Louesa I equate it very much with synesthesia—when the senses become intermingled—it's an altered state where you can hear color or smell sound. When I'm doing an arrangement I hear a melody. There's something about composition and arrangement that's like a song. There's a melody and cadence that keeps the composition from being stiff or linear. I don't think about it, I'm just in the groove, I am not conscious, I'm just feeling the materials.

A few years ago, I accidentally started collecting 19th-century European porcelain. This collection might have started with a first piece of Jasperware and next a plate of transferware and then with a short flirtation with Staffordshire porcelains. But once I discovered vases that were covered with the delicate porcelain flowers and insects that looked like they popped from a Dutch painting, I was totally hooked. The pieces that I collect are mostly from England or Germany. Sometimes I find pieces that I love at auctions but they are prohibitively expensive, so I am limited to what is affordable.

Sometimes I find a vase that I am surprised is not in a museum and feel amazed that I can buy it.

These vases are also as beautiful without fresh flowers in them. I have read that floral waters would be sprinkled onto the porcelain petals to scent a room. To me, they are a reflection of nature and botany as well as a meditation as craft, for that kind of attention to detail and beauty has my utmost respect.

Lauren McIntosh

THE EASTERN EDGE
OF THE PACIFIC

MAY

In the fields you can invent all sort of games, the ground is fresh and clean. Every so often, you can see a little mound of earth: underneath it is a mole. The light is gentle and the bushes make a pleasant shade. The ants come and go all the time along their little roads in the grass: for these ants, it is like being in a forest. What must we be like for ants? Perhaps they can't even see us. The flowers are always looking up at the sun, especially the sunflowers (except when they get it wrong and look at the moon). The poppies seem to be made of tracing paper. There are tiny little flowers which you can hardly see: some of them smell nice and the whole place smells of fresh bread.

It's great to play here and look at things . . . The field belongs to everyone, so it's ours too and we have to take care of it.

A field can be a story, the dragonfly is the most beautiful fairy, the cricket is very mysterious, the bumblebee is a wizard because he can fly without moving. The grown-ups are wolves."

L'esempio Dei Grandi—Bruno Munari

roses • philadelphus • mint geranium

It is hard to wrap your head around the scale and expanse of coastline that lies north of San Francisco. Most notable is Point Reyes National Seashore, a protected area an hour's drive north of the city in Marin County. It's a wild stretch of 80 miles, sparsely populated, and features steep, chalky sandstone cliffs that give way to stretches of sandy beaches, lagoons, and hidden coves. The area runs from Tomales Bay at the north to the Bolinas Lagoon at the southern end, which is protected by a large sandy spit that extends south to the small coastal town of Stinson Beach. Stinson is a colorful mix of old-time locals, aging hippies, and moneyed weekenders, the latter occupying the shoreline in houses that sit on the beach tantalizingly close to the water's edge, with panoramic views across the Pacific curtailed only when the fog rolls in. The rest of the town sits scattered up on the hillside above in the shadow of Mount Tam, the area's highest peak. Its full name is Mount Tamalpais, meaning "west hill;" it was named by the Coast Miwok Indians who were native to this whole coastal area before their demise, which began with the arrival of the Spaniards in 1595.

Stinson Beach is truly a remarkable meeting of the sea with the land, the town wedged between the two. The sandy beaches with tidal hot springs quickly give way to oak groves and redwoods, and it is here, halfway up the hill, that Louesa lives in a small cottage with her partner, Curtis, and Scrap, their not-so-scrappy dog, surrounded by a verdant, semi-wild, ramshackle garden and a sliver of a view of the Pacific in the distance.

Sarah

I keep finding myself living in the small and fiercely protected piece of land nestled between the gentle western slopes of Mt. Tam and the chilly Pacific Ocean. Gary Snyder calls it the eastern edge of the Pacific. Most now call it West Marin. I humbly think it is the most ideal environment I could find myself living in, at least in Northern America. I am lucky and, I guess, dedicated to living "away" for the time being.

We inhabit a very small, very sunny, very dry, and very charming 600-square-foot cottage above the town of Stinson Beach. Our little nest is part of a larger home built around 1916. The town lore is that a ship's captain lived here with his two spinster sisters. He was away at sea a great deal, so they were mostly on their own. One trip, he brought a bride home. Shortly thereafter he died, and the new bride forced the two sisters to vacate. We hear they only moved down the hill a few houses and eventually to Petaluma. These sorts of long-term rentals are the closest I know to the Holy Grail of our time period. Impossible to find, easy to love and most often providing a sense of paradise while they last. It is not hyperbole, though it sounds like stoned enthusiasm and untethered exaggeration.

Louesa

Sarah When we started this book I never imagined that roses would feature so prominently.

Louesa They're in every chapter—well, almost! There's still this idea that roses are just in the spring, but the beautiful thing about living in California is that there are roses blooming all year long. These are often the roses that have been neglected or haven't been cut back—the rogue roses. The first year I moved here I lived in Oakland and planted buttery lemony David Austin that became a huge bush, and I had beautiful roses at Thanksgiving. When you come from a different part of the country it feels like the garden of Eden here with all the lushness. It also feels wrong but in a really good way. It's disorienting to have roses in winter, but it's not out of season if the roses are blooming beautifully. A lot of how we define seasonality still comes from the East Coast and Europe, especially in the horticultural world, but if it's happening in my back yard or in a 40-mile radius then it's seasonal.

Sarah There seems to be a rose trend going on right now.

Louesa The rose of the moment is Distant Drums, which will be replaced any day with a new favorite. There are always trends as to what's in vogue or what people are obsessed with. It's the same with the food world. I love Sally Holmes, and I just bought a Hot Cocoa, but I almost feel embarrassed talking about them—I'm a rose lover, not a rose geek. I respect those who want to know every single thing about them or obsessively know every Latin rose name, but it's not how I want to approach my work. I don't want to be encumbered with too much knowledge or to think about what's in vogue or not. Partly I just want to be intuitive, and partly I just love them.

Sarah You never use gloves and happily dive into anything sharp or prickly.

Louesa I hate gloves. I don't like gear in general. I like things to be as close to the bone as possible. A glove interferes with the sense of feeling and intuition. I don't want something between me and the materials—I like the physicality of getting scraped up and hurt. The wilder the rose the thornier they are. There's something about it that's very primitive. I do wear gloves when I work with blackberries, as those thorn scratches can get infected. Blackberries, by the way, are a type of rose—you can see it in the blossom.

Sarah What is the usual cutting protocol for roses?

Louesa Cutting at an angle is good for hydrating with as much length as possible.

Sarah Good rose pairings?

Louesa We have been so indoctrinated with the idea of a dozen roses plopped in a vase by itself. What I would like to see people do is use them with other ingredients like borage or mint geranium—have one bud on its own and an arrangement of borage. Roses pair with everything to me, and we've used it throughout the book, so any of those pairings work.

Sarah How much of the leaves do you trim?

Louesa I don't trim the roses much. I trim only when the arrangement is too dense and it becomes difficult to place in or to do the composition; then I'll trim down the leaves or the thorns especially, as things can get caught up in them.

Sarah Do you have any preferences when it comes to color variations?

Louesa I try not to think too much; it's easy to have a lot of rules about palettes and color. I have my guiding preferences the same as when I paint or when doing my wardrobe. Part of me likes an all-pale creamy palette, nothing garish. That's always beautiful, but sometimes I'll want to play with crazy reds or pinks. Lately I find pale lavender roses sexy. I listen to my constantly changing sense of beauty. That's the thing with foraging and gleaning; it's not going to work for you if you decide you are going to set out and find all creamy roses. You have to be open to what you find.

Sarah Do you begin with a list?

Louesa I always have a list guided by what's in season, but I'm willing to abandon elements of the list if I don't find them and incorporate things that I come across. I begin with a concept driven by seasonal materials, and I'll think about what is beautiful at that moment. There is always an overarching list—a materials guide based on the setting and what is seasonal—but you have to be open to change in the moment. I always come back to the Chez Panisse model where the cooks write out a menu for that week, but when they go to the farmers' market and see what has come in they eliminate or add to that list based on what is most pristine and seasonal. It's the same concept with my work.

Sarah You refer to this as "flipping the list."

Louesa You can't show up and forage with a list or too many rules. When I'm doing a wedding I may have a clear idea of what I want, especially as the bride will have an idea too, but you have to be able to break the rules and use what you find. It's more challenging. I would be so bored if I just went to the flower mart, where you go and get what's on your list and it's all the same size and formula. The foraging/gleaning element forces you to think on your feet and to be creative and come up with solutions that use your intuition. I have my flora that I love to use and gravitate toward, but I always want to have my aberrations—when people get too dogmatic then the work becomes less interesting. I like to mix incorrect and aberrant with what's correct or refined. If there's a weird rose in a garish color I want to be able to use it. There's something interesting about using things that are forbidden or wrong or not on the list.

We had decided that we wanted to work with Sam Greenwood's roses—my generous friend Sam, a colleague from my early days both at Chez Panisse and then many years later a loyal supporter of my floral work. Sam has extraordinary plantings of unusual heirlooms (80 or more varieties), some carefully collected and grafted by Sam herself in her Berkeley garden. I had featured her roses before, and it was May, at the peak of their beauty. My Stinson Beach cottage seemed the perfect setting to highlight her roses again. I cut bucketfuls of her roses, mixing them with those I had in the yard and those growing in West Marin. We've recently discovered a few old remaining rose stands planted by the ranchers at the turn of the century. These specimens are extremely hardy, disease resistant, wild, brambly and overgrown, and heavily scented. We cut some of those. They add a historical element—something that has survived over sixty years untended shows that they are pretty adaptive to this environment.

SAM'S ROSES — in her own words.

The tiny purple one is 'Veilchenblau', propagated from Alice's yard, a rare blue-purple color, small blooms, climber, impressive golden stamens.

Rusty (on the left) is a variegated rusty coral color, repeat bloomer, long-lasting blooms, delicious petals.

The teeny five-petaled, blushy popcorn rose (in the small ceramics bowl) is an old rose I propagated fifteen years ago from Carrie Glen, the original florist at Chez Panisse. It is a beast that has grown to forty-five feet. It blooms once a year on great canes, each with a spray of ten to fifteen blooms that continue to bloom after being cut. The intoxicating clove scent perfumes the whole yard. When it's in bloom, the swarms of bees collecting pollen make a wonderful hum.

The stars are 'Pieter B.' (the butterscotch one, large) and Hot Cocoa (coral red). Each are repeat bloomers and huge, sometimes blooming up to five times per season. Together their antique, dusty colors are intoxicating. Coming in for the purple supporting roles are 'Othello' and Prospero, both Austin roses.

OUR TINY YARD CONTAINS ON MOST DAYS . . .

. . . honey bees, bumblebees, and wasps in great number feeding on lemon blossoms, sage blossoms, borage, lavender, decorative guava, sweet alyssum, daphne, geraniums, and in season, apple blossoms.

Here is a casually organized list of what we see and live with in Stinson. We experience very little delineation between inside the cottage and outside, except when it rains.

OUR BIRDS

Four to six hummingbirds who fight, mate, drink, perch, sing, and sleep within several feet of us, two to six very healthy crows, including one crow pair we know quite well, so well that they drink and bathe eight feet from us in the primitive birdbath we "constructed" from found materials. During the drought and heat wave they have even invited their buddies to do the same. (I wish we spoke crow.) Alligator lizards and if I'm lucky, a spring garter snake; California towhees who live in the philadelphus next to the porch; spotted towhees with their garish coats, red-shouldered hawks passing through, and slender Cooper's hawks; many bright yellow warblers flying toward the woods at the edge of Mt. Tamalpais, occasional evening grosbeaks, hermit and varied thrushes, mockingbirds, robins, of course (migrating in the spring and fall), various, rare sightings of bluebirds in the old apple trees, marsh wren, Pacific wren, and Bewick's wren, song sparrow, dark-eyed junco; noisy, nosy jays, multiple hummingbird species, kinglets, tiny dear nuthatches, phoebes, downy and acorn woodpeckers, chestnut-backed chickadees, graceful barn and cliff swallows.

OUR CRITTERS

Too may spiders to count ever, especially in the fall; slugs and snails of course, one secretive wood rat that Scrap keeps an eye on daily, pocket gophers with their many tunnels, big healthy gray squirrels who eat all the walnuts and many of the figs, foxes looking for apples mostly, stray skunks constantly wandering through, Poncho (the alley cat from across the "street"), bats (once in the bedroom), monarchs and swallow-tailed butterflies, many moths.

OUR FLORA, PLANNED AND UNPLANNED, INHERITED AND INTRODUCED

Russian sage and kitchen garden sage, borage in profusion, nasturtium, rosemary of course, adopted lavender transplants, garden variety roses I would never plant, but some I've grown to tolerate and love, one new Hot Cocoa and a Sally Holmes waiting to be planted, a huge almost brambly philadelphus (mock orange), sweet alyssum, wood sorrel (sourgrass) blanketing the yard in late winter and spring, geraniums in pots and in the ground (mostly scented varieties), passion flower vine cuttings we are propagating to be grown on the fences, a staghorn fern rescued from a hillside in Brentwood, Burmese honeysuckle, deep purple morning glories— drought tolerant— moon flowers, lemon verbena, various thymes, campanula, mints, yerba buena, red Thai and Italian basil, marjoram, fennel, dill, parsley, anise hyssop, chamomile; a very, very healthy, fruit-laden Meyer lemon mutt, pink variegated cocktail lemon struggling to live in the drought, huge healthy leggy fuzzy-leafed mint geranium and jasmine by the bedroom window, a big old rescued jade plant, potted succulents brought from LA, California poppies, wild radish, wild white onion we bring to Rintaro, hemlock galore in spring.

OUR VEGETABLES

Recently constructed raised beds under three old fruiting apple trees (that strangely bloom almost year round) containing, depending on the season—this list will grow, we hope— arugula that is now self-seeding, deep purple and red creamy new potatoes (started from Gospel Flat potatoes), tomatoes we harvest late summer into winter until November rains; kale, of course, sweet potatoes, peas, cauliflower, Bob Cannard's leeks— still babies due to our poor soil— purple basil, dill, and parsley gone to seed, coriander grown from seed, shisho, daikon, mizuna, Japanese bunching onions, and zucchini, of course.

OUR TREES

Lilly pilly tree (a myrtle tree from Australia), walnut (English), Adriatic green fig, self-seeded live oak, avocado—without a mate to fruit, awaiting two sapling baby avocado trees sprouted by Dr. Wisdom's method in South Central LA, camellia, those three very old apple trees, would like to continue adding fruit trees, as this was an orchard, and fruit is thriving due to climate change.

Candied Rose Petals or Mint Leaves

from My Pantry by Alice Waters and Fanny Singer

It is very important to taste the rose petals you plan to use, as not all rose petals have good flavor. The ideal petals taste slightly sweet and are full of aroma. Keep the rose stems in water until just before assembling these confections, which can be used to decorate cakes, served as a dessert on a candy plate, or used as a garnish on a sorbet or sherbet. They are especially pleasing with strawberry or blackberry sherbets. I use mint leaves prepared the same way to decorate a cake or to serve as candy.

Makes 50 candied petals or leaves

1 egg white

1 teaspoon water

Sugar

50 organic or unsprayed rose petals
(from 3 or 4 roses) or 50 mint leaves

In a small bowl, mix together the egg white and water until the egg white is broken up and slightly foamy. Select a pan large enough to hold the petals or mint leaves in a single layer and sprinkle the pan lightly with sugar. Have a small bowl of sugar ready, too.

Using a small pastry brush, paint each side of a rose petal or mint leaf very lightly but completely with the egg white mixture. Sprinkle each side lightly with the sugar from the bowl, so there is just a dusting one grain of sugar thick on each side. If you coat them too thickly they will be too sweet to eat and will look too crystallized. Place the coated petals or leaves on the pan to dry, taking care that the petals are not touching one another. Let them dry for an hour or two, or longer, depending on the humidity. Store in an airtight container in a cool place for about 2 weeks.

VARIATION

Any edible flower can be candied this way, as can little clusters of red currants or whole bunches of miniature grapes (also known as champagne or Corinth grapes) or gooseberries.

IN THE SHADE OF THE GRANDIFLORA

JUNE

It is Mothering Sunday, St Joseph's, Grandmother's Day. Your baby brother's first birthday, you' Mum's best friend just had a baby, it's carpenter's Name Day, uncle Giorgio has just turned up with Aunt Ester, Ines is getting married to Miro, Dante has just won the bicycle race, and Emma is getting out of hospital. As if that wasn't enough, today is the first day of Spring [. . .]. The children haven't any money, but they want to have a surprise party. So all it takes is a blade of grass and a daisy in a small jar you've just found in the games drawer. [. . .] and then you've got to arrange them; a few blades of grass, a yellow flower, a piece of moss, a glass vase, a bamboo floormat. Just like what you can see here. In the book there are lots of examples to look at, but don't just copy them.

Un Fiore Con Amore — Bruno Munari and Francesca de Col Tana

hydrangea · roses · fig · magnolia
grandiflora · queen anne's lace
wild grape · borage · blackberry

Sartorial elegance and creative careers aside—he's a photographer and she's a one-time stylist/designer— Bret Lopez and Mimi DeBlasio are not your typical Napa Valley vintners. The couple, owners of the coveted labels Scarecrow and M. Etain, were blissfully ignorant about wine when in 2002 Bret, nostalgic for the long childhood summers spent with his grandparents in Rutherford, took over ownership of their historic Victorian property on land surrounded by some of the valley's most desirable vines. The home was built in 1875, and Bret's grandfather J. J. Cohn purchased the home as a getaway from LA for his wife, Bessie. Cohn was head of MGM; The Wizard of Oz was one of the many movies he produced. When Bret and Mimi moved into the property much of Bessie's original 1940s decor and furnishings were intact: think old-world New England with a dash of forties LA, where Shaker furniture lives with Farrow & Ball striped pink wallpaper, Fortuny fabrics, and English willow-ware china.

It was midsummer when we found ourselves driving up the cherry-tree-lined driveway, arriving at the large white clapboard house overlooking the kitchen garden and circular lawn anchored by a grand magnolia tree in full bloom, with vineyards stretching into the distance. The surrounding property was bountiful

with fruit, and even early in the
day, the summer sun was already
encroaching. We headed indoors,
first setting up on the screened-in
porch, the view an impressionist haze
glimmering in the distance through
the scrim. Later, as the heat of the
sun intensified, we sought refuge
in the cool, shady 14 foot-ceilinged
rooms, taking advantage of the
interior setting, with peach-colored
walls, original strawberry wallpaper,
and furniture bedecked in floral
fabrics. We brought in towering
branches of fig and magnolia and
lengths of rose cane. The rooms
allowed for the creation of scale and
grandeur rarely afforded in a home,
with Bret's oversized photographs,
the couple's extensive art collection,
and a covetable library of art books,
creating an eclectic backdrop to
showcase the gleanings.

Sarah

and historic home, I drew upon the part of my aesthetic that was formed 42 years ago—in the South.

Magnolias—huge towering *Magnolia grandiflora*! Mimi has an unusually large and blooming specimen on the front lawn.

Fruit. The property had loads of fruit, not including the vines, which were off limits. The citrus that had been so succulent and ripe during our site visit was now dry and struggling in the heat of early summer. But as we walked the acreage we found and consumed many many plums. Famous July Santa Rosa plums and their botanical cousins were scattered about, leftovers and escapees from the turn-of-the-last-century orchards.

Bret Lopez and Mimi DeBlasio's home conjured memories, full of the golden slanted light that permeated my childhood in Lexington, Kentucky. As a child I learned a great deal about the beauty, elegance, and bucolic leisure of grand estates, usually during long old-fashioned weekends around the hunt, or the holidays, or a death or a birth. Bret and Mimi's home reminded me of all that old-world grandeur, in the wonderfully wild untamed world of California.

When I prepared my list, organized by concepts, and visually imagined what we would all create in this grand

I know it's always dicey to cut plums—the leaves wilt quickly—but the fruit and golden color was irresistible, and we were careful of rattlesnakes as we gleaned and foraged. They are an ever-present danger in the hot days' soil, leaves, and vines of Napa.

Louesa

Of course there was a rose garden. Squarely in front of that grand magnolia. It had been groomed fastidiously, so we cut kitchen-sized stems of heavenly scented and heavily petaled heirlooms. Sexy and a bit matronly, with just enough Marilyn Monroe blowsyness referencing and inspired by Mimi and her glamorous life.

Luckily there was a wilder rose hedge behind the kitchen, in a no man's land of sorts, perhaps out of the eyes of the gardeners. This huge hedge provided me with very long, tall rose canes. They were absent of blooms, but gave me the height and drama I craved. Delicate thorny canes reaching for the ceiling.

We brought borage. My intuition told me we would not find such a fog-loving "weed" in Napa in June. No formal garden would allow such a lowly thirsty weed to thrive, and it is too hot by the roads for it to survive. It did survive transport well and I love it paired with Mimi's apricot roses. We even transported a wet cold snail from Stinson Beach, hitchhiking on the same blue-blossomed borage.

Queen Anne's lace, or wild carrot, lines the roads and railroad beds in Napa and Sonoma Counties. I used to despise it actually; its relation to hemlock and a sharp odor that vaguely repels me. But Alice Waters taught me to love its structure and form, and its Victorian formality (lace) that can be loosened when used en masse. It was fitting here, and is a tough survivor in the intense valley heat, which has earned my respect. I think it pairs well with my beloved fennel, and somehow has an upstairs / downstairs vibe. Queen Anne's lace and fennel are decidedly downstairs. We all know the downstairs is more lively, sexy, yummy.

When we visit our summer home in Deer Isle, Maine, I'm struck with the imposing stands of hydrangea everywhere, in every state of care and neglect. And every shade possible, from blue to the palest citrine cream . . . like a moth's wings at night. And my perennial favorite, bloody deep (Edgar Allan Poe) scarlet, too gothic for a granite grave even. In Cape Cod I've heard there has been a civil problem with hydrangea poachers from "the city." Poachers drive in after bedtime and cut whole hedges to sell at markets. That definitely crosses the ethical line of any forager.

I was hoping for wilder hydrangea and possibly a verbena or two. But the season yielded only what welcomed us to Mimi's front door. A proper and vibrantly toned stand of healthy hydrangea. So many growing so tall that I felt no guilt as I cut and then cut some more.

MIMI D Prep for shoot June 18, 19

• Hydrangae - havent really shot well or
fully
        mimi has some and we will bring some

• Her Roses - Roses in every chapter? ha   CITRUS BLOSSOMS

• BORAGE / ROSE / HYDRANGAE   unusual combos!!   Hydrangeas
                                        Wisteria Pods

• GRAPES → Tiny if possible

• Blackberry blossoms & green fruit   - big arrangement

• Clematis ? no → SARAH ?   Magnolias
                                              dates ?   library
                                                         or
• Blue Passionflower from stinsons   living
                              ← curtis style   areas
• some more Nasturtium

ROAD • Queens Annes lace w Hydr. B fennel? Pretty
                              Big line at edge

• green fruit from Cindys? or nearby   ??

• ask Sarah - are there enough vessels ??

                                    ROSÉ
      • STRAWBERRY wallpaper - BORAGE   • LIBRARY - Meg?

SHOTS • SCREEN PORCH - Hydrangea
                                                    late day
LIST • ATTIC — BRAMBLE - Berries - Passion flower / Grapes
      • Kitchen - Mag?
      • upstairs porch @ sunset

whats going to be big? some TINY TINY here w/ BORAGE etc

Big Mag somewhere

Sarah What's it like foraging in a well-tended garden?

Louesa For me it's more gleaning than foraging, and it has a whole different emotional quality. There's so much bounty and abundance that I get excited in the moment, then the next I struggle to think of how I am going to work with everything that has been so well manicured and all cut to the same proportions. When materials are cared for so fastidiously it also forces me to be creative.

Sarah The porch was a great place to start, half indoors, half out.

Louesa To me the porch felt like old-world southern glamour. It had that languid feeling of an indoor-outdoor room. I like the thin scrim of the screen because you can kind of see the landscape but it's veiled and theatrical. It's an in-between environment so you have more freedom to behave like you are outside. Here we used huge branches of fig working with the scale and curvature.

Sarah You also mixed hydrangea with the fig.

Louesa Many people have a negative connotation with hydrangea—they associate it with dry dusty potpourri—but if you mix them with luscious moist fig branches it doesn't feel old lady and granny. There's nothing sexier than fig, with its green and curvaceous leaves—figs are a famous symbol of fertility—it takes the hydrangea to a new vernacular and gives it a different vibe and emotional quality. Persimmon, clematis gone to seed, or huge pistachio branches work well too. There are endless ways you can break up the line of the hydrangea. It's really up to you.

Sarah You like to use hydrangea in unexpected ways and pairings.

Louesa Yes, I like to use long leggy woody ones with weird wonky lines that are wild. I like the aberrations, so if I am working with the same color and range and height of hydrangea, like the ones here then I'll add texture like the Queen Anne's lace.

Sarah I like the way you juxtaposed the long rose canes with the small roses in the kitchen.

Louesa The 7-foot-long rose canes came from right outside the kitchen door at the back of the house and were a little wild and untended, while the smaller roses were from the well-tended flower beds in the front beyond the lawn. With the canes I was just responding to the architecture of the kitchen, which was tall and narrow and almost Shaker-like. They gave the arrangement structure, elegance, and height! It goes back to not liking the middle ground. If you think about it, most arrangements are a middle-size sphere or some variation of an oval ball. That's easy to do if you are working with materials all cut the same size—and that size makes it easy to transport.

Sarah You carried the canes by bending them over and holding both ends together.

Louesa Yes, I do that so that they don't whip around and cut people—or me! The canes are really malleable and surprisingly pliable when they are green and long, so they are easy to bend. It's also a way to get them through doors and spaces without knocking anything over.

Sarah This was a great place to use your trademark magnolia.

Louesa There's almost nowhere that I have worked where I didn't bring in a huge towering graceful branch of magnolia. We cut 4-foot-long branches from the tree on the lawn—putting a cross in the bottom of the cut end to hydrate the wood. The only big difficulty working with big branches is finding a vessel that doesn't fall over and crush the blossoms or make a crashing mess. If you use two or three branches they can counterbalance each other. This room received them properly.

Sarah You often talk about the importance of flora in the bathroom.

Louesa There are several reasons. One is obvious: it's good to have heavily scented flora and herbs in that room. Second, it's often the most quiet, private moment people have at an event or a dinner party, a chance to be alone and observe what's in that room. I of course like people to see and smell beautiful flora at that moment—scented geraniums, narcissus, mock orange magnolias, jasmine, gardenia, citrus blossoms, wisteria—these are some of the elements I like. Small, delicate, feminine, and lusciously scented!

THE GRIFTERS
AT THE GAYLORD

JULY

Everybody *told* me I should find romance in the West, but I hadn't expected anything so good as this . . . . a thing can't seem romantic when it's the only thing that ever happened to you . . . . And just where *have* we come? Where am I now, in respect to places one hears of— Los Angeles, for instance?

Essential Mary Austin: A Selection of Mary Austin's Best Writings — Mary Austin

magnolia • passion flower • palm dates and fruit • hibiscus • mallow • solandra • kumquat oregano • lemon verbena • shiso • basil

When Louesa talked about shooting
at the Gaylord in LA, I had blithely
thought it was a name she had
invented for the home of journalist,
author, and canning and pickling
aficionado Kevin West (author of
Saving the Season, his guide and
ode to the latter topic). It took me
a while to realize that the Gaylord
is actually the name of one of LA's
iconic buildings, a thirteen-story
1920s Italian Renaissance structure
built in Hollywood's heyday, most
recognizable by the large neon-lit
letters atop its roof, where a red-tailed
hawk or two occasionally perches.
The building lies in the heart of
Koreatown, and when we rolled
up to it in mid-July the air was hot,
fruit-stand vendors were hawking
pineapple and watermelon juices,
and the sidewalks were bustling with
people. We entered the grand lobby
of the Gaylord and navigated its
dimly lit, dusty, powder blue hallways
to Kevin's eleventh-floor apartment,
refreshingly all white and drenched
in sunlight. The one-bedroom corner
apartment, although small, offers
endless views of the city, overlooking
rows of LA's iconic palm trees,
making it feel deceptively abundant
in space.

We used the hallway corridor as
a staging ground, our buckets of
summer-colored blooms pretty
against the pale blue paint. Inside,
a tiny dining room serves as Kevin's
study, with books devoted to pure
domestic science—mostly cookbooks,
with a heavy bent toward preserves.
Louesa began placing passion flower
vines on top of the bookcase, then
wildly wrapping them around a

19th-century Eastern European painting as Kevin looked on in bemusement. Around the corner in the postage-stamp-size kitchen, packed with a mix of pickling paraphernalia and polished silver, preparations were under way for a Southern feast of sorts: pickled shrimp and country ham—a celebration of Louesa's flora with Kevin's pickles and their combined Southern heritage. To my great relief, the "country ham" was not the piece of pink plump pork I had feared, but a smooth, rich, smoky, prosciutto-like affair—a Benton ham, I quickly learned. It was beyond delicious and held its own with the sublime pickled shrimp (see recipe, p. 226). We had discussed making Bloody Marys for the shoot, an idea that quickly turned into a cocktail (see recipe, p. 226). And so, after a day of swathing Kevin's apartment in flowers and vines, we found ourselves sitting high in the sky at the end of a hot July day, homemade bloodies in hand, watching the sun slip slowly into the horizon.

Sarah

July found us hovering between seasons. I was preparing myself for a lean, slightly parsimonious hunt and installation. That is not what July in Koreatown, the Gaylord, or Mr. Kevin West gave us.

The weekend I met Kevin I was in LA for one of the early Remodelista markets. I was "between things," as people often describe a rugged midlife crisis. I packed up my beat-to-hell 1983 biodiesel Mercedes wagon (bought before the current hipster craze) with enough clothes for a month, lots of green tea, hippie snacks, and my now elderly coonhound Ida Mae. Long solitary drives on the great between lands of the I-5 had become a cathartic mix of therapy and escape from my somewhat unmoored life. A few friends were going to be part of the market, and I had few hopes besides a change of location and merchant solidarity.

As it turned out, that weekend changed the course of my life, simply by meeting three or four key people, who all saw something I didn't see in my 6-foot card table covered with a good antique textile and modest foraged flora.

Kevin West and I spoke for at least an hour that Saturday, December 10th, and I like to think there was no hidden agenda, just genuine human curiosity and connection.

In Kevin's kind words, "We both share a love of nature, the wild things that grow, and a strong sense of place. By temperament, we both tend toward nostalgia, but we're also keenly interested in engaging with the present day and progressive ideas. We share a personal and professional fixation on the specifics of place, including local history and ecology, and how both are expressed through food. We love wild edibles and other foraged/gleaned products, including flowers and natural history specimens. We both feel a connection to our deep roots in the South, but we've been shaped by our travels around the world and America. And we both found in fertile plots of land an example of how nature and the seasons overlap with culture and history at the dinner table, creating a community of people who aspire to be attuned to both the pleasures of eating (aesthetics) and the responsibilities of purposeful stewardship (ethics)."

Since that time Kevin and I have collaborated on a few events in Los Angeles. We provided carloads of herbs gleaned from the Veterans Hospital garden for a John Baldessari/Hans-Ulrich Obrist panel. About a year later we installed truckloads of wild grapes, magnolias, and roses for Kevin's book launch (*Saving the Seasons*) at the newly revitalized Grand Central Market in DTLA. Later Curtis and I lived occasionally in Kevin's apartment in the Gaylord during our early life together in California.

Louesa

The shoot began with a bit of "cheating." I had been keeping a keen eye on a long wooden wall of Prussian blue passion flower (Passiflora) growing and blooming profusely in the Stinson Beach park ranger headquarters. Really very funny if you think about it or say it out loud. My usual anxiety about not being able to source what I desired in LA emboldened me to ask the rangers if I could cut from the massive vines. John the ranger wore sweet silver dolphin earrings and had an open manner.

He readily showed us the always open rickety wooden gate, which led us into the semi-abandoned vehicle / equipment lot. Before us, on the chain link fence, grew what seemed to me endless passion flower vines in full bloom!!! We returned on the chilly evening before our drive to LA and easily and simply filled two large utility buckets with perfect specimens. I doubt we would ever find this quantity or quality of blooms in all of Los Angeles or Orange County. I had several threads running in my mind when I imagined how we would work these with our Los Angeles finds. The first look I wanted to achieve was an unexpected composition of magnolia grandiflora, arranged in a low-country,

historic manner, as a nod to Kevin's and my upbringing in the South and his recent pilgrimage to Monticello. Kevin and his partner, Braden, provided just the right amount of "camp" by bringing an all-white plaster bust of Abraham Lincoln back to the Gaylord via a cross-country car trip. His presence kept the semi-grand magnolia arrangements just silly enough for my liking.

The concept morphed from Southern hospitality to a slightly debauched beggars banquet, informed by a recent visit to the Rolling Stones photo exhibit in West LA. I wanted to take this still life to a more urbane cocktail party. We worked together without speaking, layering the country ham, farmers' market tomatoes, herbs, kumquats, solandra, and glistening fatty butter under the slightly towering magnolia grandiflora. Kevin's west-facing windows lit this very edible still life well with yellow Hollywood light.

For balance and a bit of sweet gentle femininity I often instinctively return to small, dear arrangements of seasonal herbs and roses, the more heavenly scented the better. For cocktail parties and small dinner parties they sit best in mint julep cups, cut-crystal old-fashioned tumblers, sake cups—you get the idea. The herbs should be the same herbs you are eating, the glasses the same glassware used, and the roses should never be bought!

BEGGARS BANQUET

My childhood memories of country ham share an uncanny similarity to Kevin's.

I, like Kevin, also accompanied my father to the hallowed ham house to pick up our holiday ham. My father even built a walk-in smoker behind our house to smoke pheasants, trout, pork, venison, and any game he bagged that year. I wholeheartedly agree that well-done Southern country ham rivals any smoked ham on this planet.

My father was born in Knoxville, Tennessee, to parents who both were raised in the mountains. His father was a young orphan who briefly fled west (at age fourteen) but who returned to Tennessee and Kentucky to successfully run a fine art printmaking business. His mother was more than a small percentage Cherokee, and according to family lore related to Jesse James on the Cole-Younger side of the family.

As a child in Lexington, Kentucky, and Tennessee, nearly every social gathering included a gracious, generous, formal banquet table. This table almost always included country ham, proper lard-based biscuits, and all manner of pickled peppers and vegetables, sticky cloying desserts, and free-flowing bourbon.

Louesa

THE GAYLORD

The Gaylord apartment building on Wilshire Boulevard opened in 1924. It's named after Gaylord Wilshire, who laid out the street bearing his name. The Gaylord sits across from the former site of the Ambassador Hotel, which opened in 1921 as a grand layover for socialites, moguls, movie stars, and visiting dignitaries (the LA Public Library holds menus for banquets given for Albert Einstein and General MacArthur; Bobby Kennedy was later assassinated at the Ambassador). The thirteen-story Gaylord, a towering skyscraper for its day, didn't succeed as an apartment building, even though the original Brown Derby opened next door in 1926. The Gaylord became a hotel in 1930, and compared to the grand Ambassador, it was a more modest place for writers and starlets. The fortunes of this neighborhood fell off over time, and in the 70s and 80s it became a population center for Korean and Latino immigrants. Today it's Koreatown. The Gaylord's tenants include a few very old residents who have been in their rent-controlled apartments for decades and also young artsy types. In many ways the Gaylord is the Chelsea Hotel of LA, but that gives you something of the flavor.

Kevin West

Sarah You're not a fan of middle-sized arrangements, but this was a small space and so you were somewhat contained.

Louesa Scale is relevant to the space you are working in, and because Kevin's is so small, having all those windows with no screens and the expansive sky and the views makes it feel large. It feels very indoor-outdoors in a funny way. You feel the elements up there, so that has something to do with the distorted scale. It made me want to work big in the space maybe because it doesn't feel little. I needed drama to counterbalance the all-white and clean, elemental feeling and wanted to fill the whole room with flowers.

Sarah You refer to this time of year as a scrappy time to forage. Last time we were in LA was in January and that was also a challenging month to find enough materials.

Louesa Both times there was not much going on, but the Solandra we used at Kevin's was such huge kismet. They were such an incredible Koreatown find. At Yagi's we had solandra but it perished without the sun. This time, because it was so hot, they just opened up inside at Kevin's. They're native to Mexico and love the heat and it was extraordinary to see the different shades of pale greenish yellow open up while we were there.

Sarah You were big on sourcing magnolias.

Louesa Kevin had wanted to use the magnolias, as we had foraged them before in LA for a few events we had done together. Also we have a Southern connection, and I think they are so Kevin—proper with a real formality. I didn't want this to feel like contemporary LA. I wanted it to feel like a period piece.

Sarah You brought the passion flowers with us, right?

Louesa Yes, I've discovered this huge hedge near our house and cut a couple of buckets to bring down. It's a big trip in the sun driving down I-5 to LA no matter what time of year, but I have it down now. I soak kantha quilts—lightweight ones—with water, hose down the plants, and then cover with the damp kanthas. Tea towels work too. It keeps the flowers dark and cool.

Sarah Any special tenets you adhere to when working with food?

Louesa I like there to be a common thread between the food and what flora are in season. I'll ask to see the menu if I'm doing a wedding or a dinner. I don't want the flowers to feel discordant with what is being served. I almost always use citrus in some manner, especially in LA—it feels appropriate, and it's always good when working with food as it's great in all its stages, from the green leaves, the gorgeous fragrant blossoms, to the fruit itself. The kumquats we used were found in Koreatown and were ruggedy and not pristine, but they looked good in the arrangement and added a little bit of color.

Sarah We had lots of herbs.

Louesa Yes, I brought some oregano gone to seed, and you brought lemon verbena, and Kevin bought some potted herbs. It's a good trick if you don't have herbs at hand just to buy potted herbs and, once you have chopped them down for the arrangement, plant them in the garden. We paired them with the roses—there's almost always herbs at a stage that feels seasonally appropriate.

Sarah Typically we don't bring in vessels, but for Kevin's you brought in these great tobacco colored ones.

Louesa They're ceramic insulators. I like using repurposed industrial objects as vessels— something that was pragmatic, industrial, and functional, then using it for an arrangement. The insulators are great because they are so heavy—I'm always looking for things with weight that can hold water and aren't fragile.

Sarah You had the vines extending everywhere at Kevin's—across his bookcase and dangling down, then draped over the painting. Everywhere you could.

Louesa The vines are lightweight and malleable, but sometimes I like to push out of the comfort zone of what we have been taught about flowers and how and where they should be. Who tells us these rules? At what point in our lives do we believe these rules about how big flowers are supposed to be or what vessels to use? Why can't I put flowers in insulators, or why can't they drape down the side of a painting or over the edge of the table? Why do we believe this? Who told us this? If it's your home you can do whatever your comfort level allows. Try and take things out of context. Until recently people didn't think of magnolias as flowers. Think about your space without the rules. Where can things meander and be arranged? Think about what is beautiful rather than what is proper. At Kevin's everything we did was functional. We could have had a cocktail party there . . . well, we sort of did.

PICKLED SHRIMP

from Kevin West

Along with country ham, this is another classic southern buffet food, although this one originates in the Low Country around Charleston, where the shrimp run thick in the coastal inlets come fall. It's a "pickle" because the boiled shrimp are doused with vinegar and spice. The acidity and, to a lesser extent, the spice are antimicrobial, meaning that they reduce the risk of spoilage and food poisoning. Which in turn means you can make pickled shrimp the night before and set them out on a buffet for a couple of hours without worrying they'll go off. For a very traditional recipe, consult *Charleston Receipts*, the gold standard of all Junior League cookbooks, assembled by the good ladies of Charleston in 1950 and never out of print since. Every serious Southern cook has a copy. The best homemade pickled shrimp I ever had were made by a friend of mine who comes from an old Charleston family that lives in a gorgeous antebellum house south of Broad. The secret family recipe is literally secret: only one woman per generation is allowed to see the original handwritten copy. I watched my friend make it, and the key to her version was (of all things) Wesson oil, combined in equal parts with sugar and apple cider vinegar, lightly seasoned with pickling spice and a few other things. My version for the shoot was loosely based on John Martin Taylor's recipe in *Hoppin' John's Lowcountry Cooking: Recipes and Ruminations from Charleston & the Carolina Coastal Plain*. I gave it a California spin with good olive oil, lots of lemon peel, slivered red onions, foraged wild bay leaves, and whatnot. Whatever approach you choose, pickled shrimp doesn't taste right without celery seed.

BLOODIES

from Kevin West

Why only for breakfast or brunch? A good bloody is a great cocktail to go with a Southern buffet—and it plays nicely on the savagery/ civilization theme, what with being bloody and all. I juice fresh tomatoes (tomato juice cans well, incidentally—instructions in my book, Saving the Season) and season the juice with Worcestershire sauce, plus sherry vinegar, my own prepared horseradish, homemade whole-grain mustard, homemade chipotle-based hot sauce, and a secret ingredient that I discovered on the shelf of a Koreatown market: mushroom powder, which is like umami cocaine. The seasoned base works equally well with vodka, gin, or tequila. Gin would be my pick to go with a Southern buffet. The garnish should be a homemade pickle: either a green bean, okra, or, my favorite in the context of this shoot, pickled purslane, one of my favorite weeds. All the recipes for pickles, mustard, and horseradish are in my book. They are well worth doing, because the results are so much better than store-bought. Plus, when did you ever see pickled purslane for sale? (It's an old Southern technique, though: Thomas Jefferson's distant cousin Mary Randolph included a recipe for pickled purslane in her great book, *The Virginia Housewife* from 1824.)

SKYFARING   MARK VANHOENACKER

INSIDE THE SKY   WILLIAM LANGEWIESCHE

AIR GUITAR

robert hass   what light can do

SHED

The soil is the great connector of lives, the source
and destination of all. It is the healer and restorer and
resurrector, by which disease passes into health, age into
youth, death into life. Without proper care for it we can
have no community, because without proper care for it
we can have no life.

The Unsettling of America: Culture and Agriculture — Wendell Berry

geranium • verbascum • asparagus fronds
love in a puff • clematis • roses • hydrangea
persimmon • quince • chestnut • wild grape
medlar • seckel pear • elderberry
viburnum • anise hyssop • lemon verbena
oregano • marjoram

Our impetus to shoot at SHED in Healdsburg was not simply driven by the aesthetics of the capacious glass and steel structure with its wood-lined walls and floors, the marble surfaces, and the locally made furniture, but was compelled more by what the space represented. The large white industrial-meets-agricultural market-style store with home and garden shop, restaurant, cafe, and event space is really much more than the sum of its parts. When owners Cindy Daniels and Doug Lipton created SHED in 2013, it was their way of bringing together farming, cooking, and eating under one roof. The couple, long-time locals, began their own biodynamic home farm nearby in Dry Creek Valley over twenty years ago but have been getting their hands dirty ever since they met as college students in the back-to-the-earth era in Boulder, Colorado, and their passion for food and farming has fueled their life ever since. Active in their Sonoma community, they have been bringing together farmers and chefs for a long time, but with SHED they have created a hub for the community, where 90 percent of the produce is sourced locally and events and seasonal workshops run the gamut from natural dye and cooking classes to sit-down community meals.

It was here that we created several installations loaded with late summer bounty gleaned at Doug and Cindy's HomeFarm.

Sarah

Some people see the world in grids, lines, straight streets, and graphs. Some people see the world in circles, usually radiating out from and around a nexus, and sometimes that nexus can be a moving target.

Over the course of twenty years, Cindy Daniel and Doug Lipton have envisioned, created and nurtured their HomeFarm, a biodynamic Sonoma farm of remarkable diversity, density, and beauty. A great deal of academic study (Doug has a double undergrad biology/chemistry degree, studies in agronomy at Columbia, and a PhD in soil chemistry) and years of dedicated gardening informed his dream. As a child Cindy was fascinated by seeds and seed exchanges, and this orientation is evident in many facets of SHED. After a long and thoughtful search for the correct piece of land to farm, they found a spot along Dry Creek that was flat, open and fertile, possessing rich loamy soil from the creek bed's history before the Sonoma dams.

The house was sited first, and the plan approached the entire property as if it was a garden, a mostly edible garden (edible for humans or critters). The kitchen potager came next, with two riparian corridors (moving away from the house south and east). These riparian corridors are planted and left outside of the fence to become more wild, and to create habitat and food for native wildlife. Cindy and Doug planted these corridors and meadows for birds, bees, and other beneficial insects.

Louesa

The days we were lucky enough to visit and glean we saw many, many bees, lizards, and flickers, and we were watchful of snakes. One early morning we even saw dear little bunnies, before the Sonoma heat became too intense.

Cindy is emotional, passionate, and compassionate about the soil and the critters they share this land with. One morning she spoke to me about her bees and the bee colony collapses happening in Sonoma and all over the world; tears were shed by both of us.

This commitment to deep ecology mixed with a flawless aesthetic and the vast energy to share with her community is rare and inspiring, to say the least.

We were extremely thankful and a little intimidated by the openhearted invitation to both glean nearly anything my heart desired, and then install as we wished at SHED.

I guess my gleaning followed some of the same paths that the evolution of the property took.

First I looked to the kitchen gardens to see what small, more formal plantings intrigued me. The very large, very social barn kitty, Ricky Bobby, followed and supervised this effort. It was here that I began to see some of Cindy's unexpected pairings. For instance, the hydrangea and artichokes. Not all of these companion plantings made their way into the final installations, but they all made a deep impression. We moved out towards the riparian corridor of Dry Creek and stumbled upon dramatic old rose canes that we used for the bar arrangements. Just a few feet away, my breath stopped and my heart skipped to find romantic old-world medlars and Seckel pears. I cut a few of both with great respect for the specialness of these diminutive trees.

I followed the bee meadow south, and seemed to enter into new ecosystems very quickly. Also along this more wild edge, we cut enormous healthy grapes growing into chestnut trees and anything they could attach themselves to. The birds had spread the seeds after a warm grape feast. I followed the circular paths to more arid plantings of rosemary and perhaps my favorite find of the two days of foraging and gleaning. Tall, wonky, sculptural verbascum. At first I was fooled by its velvet coat of silver green and thought it was a giant variety of lamb's ear. But it was not. Verbascum is a species of mullein native to Europe, Northern Africa, and Asia, it thrives in a hot Mediterranean climate. Cindy's extraordinary specimen had tiny tiny yellow flowers. I have a special love and admiration for mullein; it's a powerful herb to treat colds and coughs. Cindy had let these grow tall and leggy, allowing them to become curvy creatures. Perfect to me in every way.

Louesa

The adrenaline of this find pushed me south again, into the scorching heat by 10:00 a.m. We passed the olive groves and gnarly grape vines and pressed on toward the abundant herbs. The heat was already serious enough to allow only fifteen to twenty minutes of cutting at a time. It also released the intoxicating scents of lemon verbena, anise hyssop, basils of many varieties, angelica, oregano gone to seed, rose and mint geranium, and more herbs I'm sure. SHED uses large quantities of the herbs for the menus daily and for floral arrangements sold at the Grange. Fortunately for us, the heat waves of the three-year drought produced copious herb crops with little irrigation.

At one point we sought shade, again along the riparian corridor of Dry Creek. As we were eating blackberries I looked up and spotted ripe elderberry! Elderberry was on the wish list, but until that moment we hadn't found it. We were able to cut just enough to add the unusual and moody deep purple berries to the verbascum and pale pink David Austin roses arrangement that would happen later that day.

Circles. For me it always comes back to circles. After cutting a few clematis and roses at the farthest back point of the property, we circled back. Mostly because the heat had become dangerous; we needed shade and water. And we needed our newly cut treasures to survive transport. Driving now, back toward the house, we entered the huge heirloom fruit orchard. Antique peaches, Pink Lady apples, several varieties of pears, dozens of varieties of apples—hundreds of fruit trees were there for our picking.

And near the drive, Curtis and Alvaro cut grand, perfectly formed chestnut branches, full of dangerous fruit. They were sublime, possessing a deep chartreuse green and so big they required the farm truck to ferry them to SHED. Another circle we would make many times over two days, seeing new beauty and learning more of Cindy and Doug's 10-mile ecosystem with each trip.

Sarah How do you approach gleaning when all the materials are at hand? Are you more methodical in what you cut?

Louesa When confronted with formality and abundance and order, I look for the oddities, the mutants or the brambly edges. I have to organize my thoughts, have my own narrative. How am I going to traverse this landscape, then go off the path? Most of the odd things were off the path right behind the kitchen garden—the medlars and the Seckel pears and long cane-y roses that had grown huge—and there were trees that I didn't even recognize.

Sarah How do you know exactly where to look?

Louesa There is a nice cadence between the more tended garden and the edges along the creek and meadows. If you know how to focus on what is being cultivated, then on the edges it can be really wild. At HomeFarm I followed the bee corridor from meadow to creek and found some grapes gone wild, 30 to 40 feet long, growing up into the trees pollinated and spread by birds. It led me around the periphery of the property where I found elderberry to mix with the more cultivated plants.

Sarah Using herbs in arrangements is one of your trademarks.

Louesa Being edible, they're a perfect bridge between the floral and the edible world, and many herbs have flowers. I grew up with herbs used sparingly or as garnish, but herbs are very sensual, healing, and aromatic. At Chez Panisse, Alice took herbs to a new level and used them in abundance—she's famous for developing people's deep love for herbaceousness.

Sarah You particularly like to use herbs gone to seed.

Louesa That goes back to liking things that are not over-manicured. People tend to think of herbs as uniform, a certain size and scale, like basil and oregano trimmed in a kitchen garden, but if you let them go to seed in the fall they get tall, leggy, and wild. California was the first place I ever saw this. If you let them do their thing naturally, you'll get the wonky lines and curvature, and they're more luscious and scented this way. You still want to cut them back in the winter, but I like to let mine go to seed first.

Sarah The silvery verbascum were a great find, deceptively wobbly to hold.

Louesa Yes, it's some kind of giant species—the grandiflora of verbascum. They're so Dr. Seuss-like and curvaceous, a life force, and they looked so out of context in the grassland setting—more like a Mexican cacti. Everything is bigger here in California. They're so fragile you have to transport them one at a time. I put them in a kantha quilt, separated to keep the shape and protect the little yellow blossoms and seed pods.

Sarah You have been really inspired by some of Cindy's floral combinations in her garden.

Louesa I rarely borrow directly from other people, but I did from Cindy's pairing of borage and butterscotch roses, and the idea of using verbascum with the dusty pink roses was also directly inspired by her. I am always making decisions based on how people have combined their materials in the garden, so Cindy's aesthetic comes through in my work.

Sarah The 18-foot ceilings upstairs at SHED provided plenty of space but were also a challenge to work with.

Louesa I knew I wanted a spherical structure to hang things from, because the logistical challenges of the height in that room made it dangerous to work with. I had seen the wooden sphere around the garden—a Burning Man relic that Tim [my landlord] had made. He let me borrow it, but I had no idea what we would hang. I was thinking herbs, and we had talked about verbena, but it was too stiff and linear. That's when we thought to use the love in a puff; it's more tendril-y and viny, easier to twist and drape and get that waterfall effect. We added clematis too, but not much.

Sarah We also used the asparagus fronds.

Louesa Yes! I love, love, love them, but you don't find a lot in California. The asparagus had gone to seed, and the pieces were easy to hook over the sphere. We kept layering so they were almost all going in the same direction, like in a garden or meadow. You want a teeny bit of human hand but not manipulated to the point that it looks vastly different from in nature.

Sarah What are the challenges of working with scale in a retail space?

Louesa Working on such a big scale drew upon my work at the restaurant Bar Agricole. SHED has a similar austereness and really big-scale beautiful architecture. I arranged the piece jenga-style on a grand scale. People are afraid of that scale, but there are ways to make it safe with counterweighting and knowing the limits of a vessel. Usually tall and skinny compositions are good, so I like to use willow, bay, or magnolias without a thick, heavy branch. You want the scale to happen above people's heads, and the chestnut here was great for that. I often cut off what is dangerous at hand or eye level and keep everything above head level. I always want to push the limits, and a lot of people say there is a little bit of danger in my work, but people have to be comfortable.

Sarah We went from oversized to super small.

Louesa I like to start big, then break things down into smaller and smaller parts—a snout-to-tail approach. All the materials were reused flora placed in the little brown glass vials. It was just another integration between HomeFarm and SHED. It's all of the same piece—a full circle.

EPILOGUE

Beauty is a terrible and awful thing! It is terrible because
it has not been fathomed and never can be fathomed,
for God sets us nothing but riddles. Here the boundaries
meet and all contradictions exist side by side . . .

The Brothers Karamazov — Fyodor Dostoevsky

———————

Of all mediums, flora is the most ephemeral, the most fragile, the quickest to deteriorate,
decompose, dry, wither, and die. Unlike most of my peers, I don't believe in or spend time
trying to slow this natural process. I find it fascinating, moving, and utterly beautiful.

All talented floral designers take great pride in creating romantic, lush weddings. But I am
curious why these same designers don't want to create hauntingly beautiful funerals, an
equally important ceremony in this life! I do. I would love to create a whole new genre of
incredibly thoughtful, dark, brooding, and personal memorial flora.

As we began to close down a year of shooting (twelve shoots over as many months), I
desired to document some of the memorable material we had used in a state of decay.
I often bring bits, remnants, and treasure from gigs and shoots into the house—like
a crow—and we watch them dry and decay, set amongst the beach stones, collected
feathers, bones, lichens, trinkets, and miniature relics that make up our living space.

I had amassed a little collection of one or two things from each shoot, and I wanted
to photograph and document these as a funereal record of the year.

SELECTED FLORA

FENNEL – FOENICULUM VULGARE – ANGIOSPERMA

This family owes much of its beauty to multiple masses of tiny florets in various shades of yellow or bronze, with great variety depending on the stage of its yearly life cycle. Fennel is in the sea botanical family that includes dill (of course), carrot, parsnip, parsley, and the infamous and deadly hemlock, which is native here in California.

Fennel is native to southern Europe and the Mediterranean, where it has been used for many many centuries as a culinary treasure and prized medicine. Speculation is that it was introduced to California about 120 years ago and thrives in our mesic locations with our Mediterranean climate, colonizing from sea level to 2,000 feet. This beautiful "weed" prefers and thrives in disturbed areas, especially weedy areas near fresh or brackish fresh or salty water. It grows tall and abundant in pasture, abandoned lots, roadsides, and open banks of creeks, estuaries and bays. You can see why I love it!!

The "fennel" we often use is not a true fennel. *Ferula communis*, giant fennel, is a California native growing 6 to 8 feet tall.

Fennel will reproduce from both taproot and seeds, which are dispersed by water, birds, rodents, even vehicles and clothing. Hence the moniker "invasive." Flower production usually begins when the plants are eighteen to twenty-four months old. Germination can occur at any time of the calendar year. Flowers may be seen from early spring to late late fall, making it especially useful for my work.

In medieval Europe, fennel wreaths were hung above doorways on midsummer days to keep "witches" away.

In the Pyrenees, fennel fronds were fastened to rooftops for protection against evil magic.

In order to invoke rainfall, the ancient Phoenicians planted fennel in clay pots around the image of the god Adonis. The rapid sprouting of the seeds, fast growth, and subsequent withering of the sprouts in the heat were symbolic of the death and resurrection.

Roman warriors consumed fennel seeds, often mixed with honey to increase fighting strength, stamina, and courage, and fennel victory wreaths were worn after victories.

The Romans had at least twenty-two medicinal uses for fennel, including but not limited to snake bites, insect repellent, calming of the bronchial tubes, mouth health and odor, tonics for liver, kidney, and spleen, and indigestion.

Some of the medicinal benefits include:

high levels of flavonoids, antioxidants, phenylpropanoids

anti-inflammatory properties

high concentrations of minerals (copper, iron, niacin, calcium, potassium, manganese, selenium, zinc, and magnesium).

vitamins A, E, C, and B complex

Ayurvedic properties

A most divine herb to me.

QUINCE – CYDONIA OBLONGA FLOWERING QUINCE –CHAENOMELES SPECIOSA

The common quince is a 10-foot tall, crooked-branched tree native to western Asia with four known species in temperate climates grown for its incredibly fragrant fruit. It has also been used throughout eastern and western civilizations for jellies, preserves, compotes, and pies traditionally eaten at Christmas time. The fruit must be cooked for human consumption.

The *Chaenomeles* species (Asiatic) are self-sterile, hence requiring multiple trees for fruit production. Slow growing and long lived, these diminutive trees are set at one to two years, with fruit beginning to bear at three years.

Chaenomoles speciosa is the earlier flowering and most spectacular, as it blooms early in the spring before the leaves appear.

Chaenomoles japonica flowers later, with its leaves, and then again often in the fall.

The scent of both fruits is so heavenly that it was a custom in medieval and Shakespearean times to place the ripe fruit in drawers and wardrobes, scenting linens and garments.

I know from my own experience that a single fruit in a bowl will scent an entire room!

Quince branches are an excellent choice to bring spring blossoms into the home. If cut before flowers appear, they will force in the heat of the house and keep blooming for two to three weeks.

MAGNOLIA

Magnolias have been on this earth a very very long time. Fossils of flowers date back to at least before the Cretaceous period, in the time we know as the age of the dinosaur (144–65 million years ago).

Fossil flowers that are nearly 100 million years old, found in what we now call North America, look remarkably like today's magnolias. Truly native!

The flowers of magnolias are central to the development of ideas about the first angiosperms, flowering plant. Both sexes are present in this flowering tree. They are among the first of all known flowering plants, yet more specialized and complex than blooming grasses or wind-pollinated flora.

MAGNOLIAS, BEES AND BEETLES . . .

Beetles share a special relationship with magnolias. They are attracted to the heavily and heavenly scented flowers and bumble into and over them, clumsily eating the anthers full of nitrogen-rich pollen. Secretions from the petals and formal parts of the flower collect on the beetles' bodies, which they then carry to the next magnolia they visit. Interspecies sex! The magnolias avoid self-fertilization because the male and female bits of the flower have distinct and different phases in different times of the year. Very smart. Magnolias' flowers thus predated bees on this planet!

Who's to say, given the ancient history of magnolias, whether they truly are 'native'?

They currently populate Asia (from the Himalayas to Japan), the Americas, and most of Europe. They most likely were introduced to Europe in 1688. The name hails from Pierre Magnol, French Huguenot botanist (1638–1715).

The Chinese attribute many medicinal properties to magnolias. The thick bark is used as a tonic (some barks even smell of citrus); the petals are consumed to treat colds, fevers, and allergies.

Over the years I have heard of a few recipes involving magnolia.

As a blond blowzy woman driving a red convertible once saw me cutting them (with permission!) in the only 7-Eleven in tony Mill Valley, she claimed that as a younger person in the Deep South she drank magnolia cocktails. I also found a few Japanese pickled magnolia recipes.

There are eighty-five or more subspecies of magnolias; a few I like to use include:

Magnolia grandiflora (southern magnolia), sometimes referred to as laurel leaved tulip tree.

Magnolia x *soulangeana*

Magnolia liliiflora

Magnolia denudata – Yulan magnolia, Japanese name Haku-mokuren

Magnolia globosa – globe flowered

Magnolia campbellii (Campbell's magnolia) found in the mountains of China; used to make tea boxes.

PEONY OR PAEONY – PAEONIA

"It is worth while selling everything one possesses to buy peonies and to dig up everything else in the garden to make room for them." Attributed to a master gardener named Coats.

Another historical quote from American author Richardson Wright:

"The fastest way to financial ruin is to have a personal propensity for indulgence in tree peonies."

A poem by Po Chu-I (722-846)

"100 pieces of damask for the most beautiful flowers, 5 pieces of silk for the more common types. A bunch of dark red peonies would pay the taxes on ten poor people's houses."

These quotes begin to describe many people's deep deep love of peonies; they also describe why I am often conflicted when using them, and will never pay or participate in the paeonia trade out of season and from far away.

That being said, they are remarkable, and we were careful to use peonies grown as close as possible, from a biodynamic farm, and in season!!

There are twenty-five to thirty species in this genus, and they are found throughout the Pacific coast of North America, Asia, and Europe—wild peonies grow in Italy!

The history of peonies follows two separate branches:

The western species (*Paeonia officinalis*), which has chiefly medicinal properties.

The Chinese species (*Paeonia lactiflora*), grown since at least the 5th century BCE.

Tree peonies have been cultivated in Asia for over fifteen hundred years, with more than three hundred varieties in all shades of the rainbow.

There are also intermediate gradations of all colors and striped and bicolored forms.

The mythology of Europe's Paeonia officinalis is extensive. It was said to be an important part in "horrible mixtures and potions brewed by witches and sorcerers" (*Flowers, A Guide for Your Garden*).

Paeonia was derived from Paeon, who with a poultice (that of course included *Paeonia officinalis*) healed Hades of a wound inflicted by Hercules.

Pliny the Elder was said to have written extensively of its many healing properties. Pliny wrote that it was necessary to gather the plant furtively at dusk, taking great care not to be seen by the green woodpecker, who would attack the gatherer and poke out his eyes! Very dramatic indeed.

PASSION FLOWER – PASSIFLORA

Most people would never think of using passion flower vines or blooms in arrangements. But over the course of my life in California, it's become one of my most favorite things in the entire world. It's like it's from another world, the sea, or another planet.

The story of how (over five hundred subspecies) of Passiflora came to "The New World" is typically colonial and Christian, common to many botany treatises before this century:

"In the year 1610, the Roman theologian Giacomo Bosio received a visit from an Augustine friar who had recently returned from Mexico.

This friar presented Bosio with a drawing of a flower so unusual and marvelous that Bosio called it the most extraordinary representation of the cross triumphant ever discovered in field or forest. The flower contains within itself not only the savior's cross but the symbols ōf his passion." Hence its European moniker.

The Spanish colonists in Mexico and Central America call it the flower of the five wounds owing to its complicated structure.

Native to many parts of the southern hemisphere and the southern temperate climates of the United States (it is the state flower of Tennessee), it is often referred to as tender, but in fact is quite vigorous and resilient, an aggressive climber that blooms during multiple seasons, at least here in California. There are at least twenty species that thrive in the Americas, with shades of pure white, pale greenish white, cerulean blues, deep purples, bloody reds, bright oranges, and pale pinks and yellows.

I find great beauty and value in all parts of this plant—vines, blooms, and fruit. The fruit of passiflora ligularis is called granadilla and in addition to being delicious and versatile, contains many health benefits: antioxidants, minerals, vitamins, and fiber.

Passion flower has gained modern medical attention for its use in treating anxiety, insomnia, depression, and menopause.

Maybe it does contain sacred powers.

SOLANDRA

Solandra is a native to Mexico; it was and possibly still is used by the Huichol people. It is a sacred medicine; archeological evidence supports the theory it predates peyote. It is distant cousin to datura, another sacred hallucinogen. The blooms last only one or two days if you are lucky. I prefer to force them indoors as we

did at Kevin West's shoot, where they began as pristine blooms and decayed more slowly. It is extremely poisonous, so exercise caution.

BORAGE

Also referred to as Starflower, in the flowering plant family of Boraginaceae. Native to the Mediterranean, anything that grows there grows well in California.

Flowers vary from vibrant "Delphinium" blue, to pinkish purple, and more rarely, a pale white. Cooked, the thistle portion of the plant has a cucumber or cardoon flavor with a sweet tasting flower. Like nettles, it's often used as a filling for ravioli, and is the traditional ingredient and garnish for a Pimm's cup cocktail. It also often flavors gin. It makes an excellent honey, as the bees adore it.

Borage makes an excellent companion plant alongside tomatoes, cabbages, and other crops, helping to ward away insects and worms. It is also said to improve the yield and disease resistance of the companion plants.

Borage was sometimes called *bugloss* by the old herbalists. A hardy annual coming originally from Aleppo. High in potassium and calcium, with mineral acids. "The flowers candied and made into a conserve, were deemed useful for persons weakened by long sickness and for those subject to swoonings….." A Modern Herbal.

It's also a prolific spreader! It's a useful plant, which dyes garments a bright blue and beekeepers grow it to help bees produce more honey!!

Italian grandmothers coat the leaves in breadcrumbs and fry them, then serve with risotto – or stuff the leaves with cheese, bread, and fry.

Pliny the Elder claimed borage was used to "exhilarate the mind, comfort the heart, drive sorrow away, and increase happiness."

ELDERBERRY

"When you settle a share of land, first plant an elder tree, then make your home there." T. Elder Sachs

Sambucus is in the genus of flowering plans in the family *Adoxaceae*. It was formerly placed in the honeysuckle family (Caprifoliaceae) but was reclassified due to genetic and morphological comparisons to Adoxa.

There are twenty-five to thirty species of this deciduous shrub, small tree, and herbaceous perennial plant, which grow in temperate to subtropical regions and thrives in Mexico.

Large clusters of white delicate panicles of small white or cream flowers bloom in late spring often seen along streams, edges of the forest, and roadsides.

Then we see displays of glorious clusters of small bluish-black purple, red or black berries in early fall. Very rarely the fruit is yellow or even white.

Elder identification is extremely important!! To the untrained eye it may resemble deadly hemlock, pokeberry, or other poisonous plants.

The plant has been called the 'medicine chest of country people' by none other than Hippocrates in 400 BCE. Both the white delicate panicle flowers and the deep almost blue-black berries are used for culinary and medicinal uses, the stems, leaves and bark are toxic.

Fresh flowers harvested in spring are used for the distillation of elder flower water.

It is now widely accepted even among western allopathic medicine as an effective prevention and treatment for influenza, reducing duration and severity. Also used commonly for colds and other respiratory conditions including bronchitis. Very effective as a treatment for children's coughs, as a syrup is easy to take, digest, and yummy.

Has antifungal, and anti-mold properties.

All parts of the plant are a valuable addition to the compost heap and improve fermentation.

A beautiful rich dye can be obtained from the fruit and more mature bark. The leaves produce a vibrant green dye and the berries, of course, rich hues of blues and purples.

Elderberry also contains a very high oxygen radical absorbance capacity, twice that of blueberries or cranberries, more vitamin C than oranges, and high levels of antioxidants (this comes from the plant's defense mechanisms to survive high levels of UV light from direct sun). All of these result in a powerful healing ability that support immune health, brain function, and provide anticarcinogens.

In addition to the positive and beneficial relationships between humans and elder, there is some darker lore. Some legends claim that elderwood was used both for the 'cross' of Jesus Christ and that Judas hanged himself from an elder tree. A myth that persists. Like many powerful plants, some patriarchal cultures claimed 'witches' would gather under the plant, especially when it's full of fruit. Probably just herbalists collecting berries!

If an elder tree was cut down, a spirit known as the elder mother would be released and take her revenge. The tree could only be safely cut while chanting a rhyme to the elder mother.

A little more:

If you do need to cut some wood from the tree, approach the tree with respect; ask first, and listen with an open heart. Don't cut if you get a strong intuition not to. Some

people like to leave a small gift of some kind - something practical, like untangling ivy, from around the trunk, watering in dry weather, or tidying up rubbish from around the tree. An attitude of gratitude and thanks to the tree is a positive act to which all of nature responds well. Others say it matters not to the tree, but the very act of thanking opens up something in us which is very healthy and necessary for our spirit. For this reason, it is important to state your thanks simply, and from the heart, each time you take nature's gifts. I also find that it builds up a bond with a tree, a friendship of great power and wisdom. The Elder, of all the trees, has much to teach us, through direct contact, communication, and reconnection to past uses and lore.

One note: Due to the extreme drought of the past few years in California, we sadly didn't get to include elderberry flowers and berries as much as I wished in this book! A lesson about the tenuous relationship we all share with nature and beauty! There are some sweet bits of elderberry in Shed.

NASTURTIUM

Tropaeolum minor – Greek for "to twine." At least 50 species of nasturtiums. They are in the same family as watercress, mustard, and cabbage, the family known as *Brassicaceae*. The name comes from the Latin 'Nasus Tortus' (twisted nose), a funny image of the feeling we get when we consume too much mustard or wasabi.

In West Marin this lush, edible plant literally grows by the roadside, creeks, covers vacant lots, and easily establishes itself in most yards. The leaves have become one of my favorite shapes in nature and resemble translucent brilliant green water lily pads. Occasionally the leaves are variegated, or speckled.

The blossoms appear delicate but in fact are quite hardy and super

delicious! There are hybrids, which possess more unusual coloration, such as the vermillion "Empress of India," peach melba, butter cream, tangerine, all edible names. I have a theory that these 'exotic' varieties often revert to our 'common' nasturtium colors. I love them all equally.

They take over!! Something I value and many gardeners fight year after year, but happily the nasturtium always win this battle.

They originated from Peru and other regions of South America.

As it seems to be with many medicinal herbs, the native people of Peru used the leaves and flowers to treat coughs, colds, flu, and women's health. In Ayurvedic medicine the leaves are rubbed on the gums to stimulate and cleanse the mouth.

I treasure nasturtium for their twirly elegance and fresh beauty that I think is often misunderstood and misused. They are perfect for long, tendrily ikebana-style arrangements, we often bring just one long vine into the house. We also demonstrate how they can be used en masse, resembling how they grow by the roads, tall and rambly. Sadly, most florists use them small, often in mason jars, which doesn't show off this sweet plant's architecture.

ACKNOWLEDGMENTS

SARAH

Thank you to our editor, Jenny Wapner, for your stellar counsel and guidance in bringing this book to fruition and to the entire team at Ten Speed Press for their support.

Huge thanks to our photographer, Laurie Frankel, who showed unwavering devotion to this project, going above and beyond, and who shared her outstanding eye in documenting the flora in this book. Thanks also to her studio—Gary Beberman, Aly Su Borst, Jen Laggin and Julius, and her crew—Brian Slaughter, Aaron Fee and Trever Gens.

Many, many thanks to Curtis, who was with us from the very beginning and whose help has been boundless.

One of the greatest joys in creating this book was collaborating with friends who generously opened up their homes to us, even when we were high on concept and short on detail. We are indebted, and thank you for entrusting us not only with your homes and workplaces, but often allowing us to use your extraordinary vessels and objects. Your kindness was instrumental in the creation of this book. Thank you to you all: Tori and John Williams, Richard Carter, Heidi Swanson and Wayne Bremser, Luc Chamberland, Tamotsu Yagi, Sylvan Mishima Brackett and the crew at Rintaro, David Hoffman, Lauren McIntosh and Stephen Walrod, Mimi DeBlasio and Bret Lopez, Kevin West, Cindy Daniel and Doug Lipton, Mark Evans and Charley Brown.

There are always more people to thank and the following were generous enough to contribute in some way, whether it was providing flora, vessels, recipes or just plain manpower. Thank you: Sharon Jones, Bob Cannard, Kelly Farley, Patrick Martin of Putah Creek Hops, Molly Prier, Yuko Sato, June McCrory, Martin at The Last Resort, Nick Walrod and Dancing Moon Farm, Norma Listman, Liz Pruitt, Samantha Greenwood, Fanny Singer, Todd Nickey and Nickey Kehoe, Alvaro Sayago and Inocensio Gonzales at HomeFarm.

Thank you to Louesa whose propensity for expansiveness opened my own horizons.

Most importantly, thank you to my family, David, Conrad, and Imogen who are always supportive of my endeavors, this book not withstanding, and who no longer bat an eye when I wrangle a ridiculously oversized branch or piece of flora into our home.

LOUESA

For me any formal public acknowledgment should begin with my mom, and then probably my grandmother and great grandmother. My mom kept an artful, thoughtful, warm home full of beautiful food, objects, textiles and color and when possible in Ohio, flowers. She has an innate sense a balance and restraint with a generous spirit (and thank you Jim Creek for taking such good care of her).

My dad imparted his Cherokee heritage, including the coyote trickster ways. Truly looking, seeing, observing and loving the natural world around us, right in front of us. Simply and intensely learning to look more closely. He taught me why that was valuable and spiritual, and how most people in our culture don't access this part of our being, our brains, or spirits nearly enough.

I want to thank Joshua Roebuck, he has and always will stand beside me in my life. The Roebuck clan brought me to California, and have had untethered enthusiasm and love for every creative incarnation. He and they have been a source of unconditional love, steady support, and humor over the past twenty-five years of my being a lucky member of the family.

I will always be informed by and thankful for my first California community of Chez Panisse. Many thanks to all the friends from Chez Panisse who reabsorbed me after the financial collapse of 2008 who saw and understood what I was doing and why it made sense as a continuing part of the local ecological narrative: Sylvan Mishima Brackett, Kelsie Kerr, Samantha Greenwood, and many more.

And also Erica Tanov for letting me continue to grow in my new aesthetic landscape. Thank you to Tim Dawson for the chance to live on the western edge of Mt. Tam—I knew that first bright clear October moment I stood in the garden it was a perfect nest.

At that same time in my life, Evan Cole saw and understood a great deal from a modest card table of my early work and offered a tiny, neglected rug closet for me to turn into a little showcase for my unusual foraged floral work. A place to manifest for a little while. And most importantly a space to meet people who would change the course of my life.

Of course, Sarah Lonsdale also saw something which resonated with her, and it's still a fruitful dialogue.

Laurie Frankel wandered into that little shop on Hayes and we recognized kindred spirits in each other instantly.

Thank you Jenny Wapner for asking me more than once to collaborate, your mind and wise insight enabled me to say yes to this book. Matthew Baker has almost always been next to me, every time I try to take this crazy labor intensive, physically demanding, non-formulaic way of creating flora to the public. He has been my good fairy every time with his truly magical critter ways... I hope I have been as loyal and inspiring.

Scrap, the best helper.

Alvaro Sayago and Inocensio Gonzales, who are such competent loving stewards of Cindy and Doug's HomeFarm.

Kevin West, offering shelter and collaboration, and a shared history of the gracious Smokey mountain regions of the last century, something few have memory of these days.

And, with all my heart, I thank Curtis Searle Fletcher for finding me after looking in Columbus Ohio, New York City and many other places. Thank you for making your home with me beside the mountain and by the sea and wherever we lay our heads. You have given me and this creative endeavor your entire being, and more I think, for two years. You see more than I do, and now we see and create together.

"Peace is the breath of stones, stars and sages."—Paramhansa Yoganada

INDEX